SCREAM

DECONSTRUCTED:
AN UNAUTHORIZED ANALYSIS

SCOTT KESSINGER

Stinger Books
Las Vegas, NV
stingerbooks@gmail.com

ISBN-13: 978-0615545790
ISBN: 0615545793

CONTENTS

CONTENTS, Cont.

ACKNOWLEDGMENTS

For providing support, inspiration and/or insight:

- ♦ John Klyza

- ♦ Adam Bertocci

- ♦ The community of *Scream* fans

- ♦ Of course, the cast and crew of the *Scream* films

de·con·struct

verb *dē-kən-strəkt*\

transitive verb

1: to examine (as a work of literature) using the methods of deconstruction

2: to take apart or examine in order to reveal the basis or composition of often with the intention of exposing biases, flaws, or inconsistencies

3: to adapt or separate the elements of for use in an ironic or radically new way

—Merriam Webster

Introduction

If there were only a single word available to describe the movie *Scream,* I would use "seminal." If the movie has done anything to popular culture, it's start things.

Most any genre fan will recall that *Scream's* success kick-started a horror movie revival in the late 1990s after nearly a decade of dormancy for the genre, but its influence has spread even further than that. After *Scream's* success, Hollywood figured if the 80s teen slasher could make a comeback, then maybe the 80s teen gross-out comedy could make a comeback as well, leading them to take a chance with *American Pie,* an R-rated teen comedy whose own success brought on a trend of raunchy teen flicks in the early 2000s and, then later, adult comedy in general.

The *Airplane!*-style spoof also got a jumpstart when 2000's *Scary Movie* saw huge box office returns. *Scary Movie* was a low-brow parody of the *Scream* films that coincidentally (or not?) shares the title of *Scream*'s original script. Horror, raunchy comedies and spoofs: that's three whole film genres who can thank *Scream* for their revival.

But perhaps even more importantly, *Scream* invited a whole generation of movie fans to start viewing film in a more critical light. Popular online magazine *The A.V. Club* even pronounced *Scream* a "Gateway to Geekery." Not only were more people introduced to the horror film through *Scream*, but to the idea that the horror film could be about more than a masked killer with a knife or a monster in the shadows. In fact, *any* movie is much more than the sum of its parts.

And that, ultimately, is what this book is about. Movies, like any art form, say things, and these pages are devoted to interpreting just what the *Scream* films—the four of them made as of this writing—are saying. If "reading" films is already a hobby of yours you'll no doubt get a kick out of this or perhaps confirm your own theories. *Scream* aficionados should enjoy venturing into the films' psyche. It's my personal hope, too, that after reading this a novice film junkie gets inspired to analyze more of their favorite movies, because every movie says *something*.

I want to stress that many of the themes outlined in this book are subjective and are not meant to put words in the mouths of the filmmakers, be it Wes Craven or Kevin Williamson or Ehren Kruger. We can speculate if the themes in the *Scream* films are intentional or otherwise influenced by their personal perspectives and experience, but in the end, it's up to the viewer to find meaning in a work. Indeed, *Scream*'s core message seems to be just that exactly: that the meaning the recipient finds in a message is more important than the one the messenger intends.

What makes *Scream* such a fun and ideal "Introduction to Film Theory 101" subject is that, in all honesty, *Scream* isn't a tough movie to figure out. I'm not claiming at all to be a genius for being able to write an entire book about *Scream*. But it's this very accessibility that makes it easy to overlook the depth of the movie's themes—or worse, misunderstand them. In spite of their enormous financial and critical success, I think the *Scream* films are actually *underrated* in some circles.

Depending on his or her background or disposition, some of the things in this book may make perfect sense, seem obvious, or seem outlandish or over-reaching. But it should be noted that, unless specifically qualified as a personal pet theory, everything in this book is supported by what happens on the screen, which is fitting because according to *Scream*, what's on-screen is nearly as important as what happens in real life.

Part I—
SCREAM

What the Hell is It?

It's interesting to note the variety of answers you'll get in response to the question "What's *Scream* about?" Depending on who you ask, the most likely response would probably be one of the following:

- ♦ *It's about a guy in a mask that kills people with a knife.*
- ♦ *It's a horror movie about horror movies.*
- ♦ *It's a parody of horror movies.*
- ♦ *It's a mystery thriller.*
- ♦ *It's a dark comedy.*

When we examine these explanations closer, we find they have varying degrees of accuracy:

"It's about a guy in a mask that kills people with a knife."

This is easily the most literal of the explanations, but even this misses the mark in ways that aren't insignificant. *Scream* certainly has a guy in a mask that kills people with a knife, but *Scream* is much more about the people he stalks than it is about him.

And while we're on the subject of literal plot synopses, it's about time I provide one myself, though if you're reading this without having seen any of the films you should probably drop this book and track down a copy to watch before this book blows all their secrets for you. The *Scream* series revolves around Sidney Prescott, who we follow from high school to adulthood, and a core group of her friends, acquaintances, and enemies—most notably police officer Dewey Riley, tabloid journalist Gale Weathers, and movie geek Randy Meeks—as they are stalked by a masked serial killer (a different killer for each film) inspired by horror movies.

That's all surface, though, all text. The juicy stuff is when we get to the *subtext*.

"It's a horror movie about horror movies."

Here we're starting to get into the "twist" of *Scream*. One of the great pleasures of the *Scream* films is that its characters have seen other horror movies. In fact, some of them are straight-up genre buffs that are intimately familiar with the slasher setup and formula. In this way and others, *Scream* is indeed a horror movie about other horror movies and so this explanation gets points for accuracy, if not completeness.

"It's a parody of horror movies."

This one, I feel, is a common misconception. The sentiment that *Scream* is a parody of slasher films was born from the descriptions of the movie using the term "parody" as shorthand for *Scream's* (a) referencing horror movies and (b) moments of lighter tone and comic relief.

There are plenty of witty one-liners and lighter character bits in *Scream*, but there really aren't a lot of out-and-out *jokes*, and when there are the jokes aren't usually at the horror movie genre's expense (the one big, giant exception here being *Stab*, the film series within the film series that mimics the events of *Scream*, only in a much schlockier form).

Parodies usually work by exaggerating the features and faults of its subject into ridiculous comic oblivion. There's no scene in *Scream*, for instance, in which a buffoon-ish character is startled by a jumping cat in his bathtub (or some other unlikely place) in order to get the audience to laugh. In fact, the only time *Scream* does deploy the old leaping-cat-fake-out-jump-scare, it's done with the utmost sincerity!

Putting the kibosh on whether *Scream* is a spoof or not is the fact that it was able to support a parody of its very own: the aforementioned *Scary Movie*, a comedy in the Abrahams and Zucker tradition of absurd gags and the ridiculous exaggeration that is absent in *Scream* itself.

Another word that gets brought up a lot in regards to *Scream* is *satire.* Because 'satire' is one of those words whose meaning gets distorted from conversation to conversation like a game of telephone, we'll double-check with Webster's: satire is "the use of irony, sarcasm, ridicule, or the like, in exposing, denouncing, or deriding vice, folly, etc."

Here I think we're getting closer to the mark. *Scream* is certainly ironic, it references horror movies, and seeks to advocate for their improvement (I'll get to that later). Also, the satire label does not have the stringent requirements on jokey-ness the way a parody does.

There's a certain mean-spiritedness inherent to satire, though, that isn't quite there with *Scream*. Oh, *Scream* has a mean streak alright, but not really in regards to the subject of horror movies, which would theoretically be on the receiving end of *Scream*'s satirical edge. Some of *Scream*'s characters may cry out how they hate that horror movie "shit," but *Scream* really wants nothing if it doesn't want the horror film genre to be taken seriously.

So *Scream* has some of the intentions of a satire without necessarily the spirit. The "satire" description, then, gets a resounding affirmation of: "kind of."

"It's a mystery thriller."

Most slasher movies live or die by their "Final Girl" sequences: the climactic chase scene in which the last surviving protagonist (virtually always a female) finally kills or escapes from the killer. The rest of the movie usually consists of filler and the occasional memorable death.

The standard slasher movie stalk-and-kill scene usually plays out something like this:

A young woman investigates a strange noise in the middle of the dark.

"Jimmy, is that you?"

She hears the noise again.

"Jimmy, this isn't funny anymore!"

The score hits a STINGER as THE KILLER pops up into the scene.

"AAAAAAUUUGGH!"

The killer stabs the woman, there's a lot of blood, and the film cuts to the next scene.

Not so with *Scream* (at least, not usually). You could even say the *Scream* movies consist entirely of Final Girl sequences: they're chock full of chase scenes, clever set pieces, and victims that try to fight back against the killer.

People forget that *Scream* was originally marketed as a *thriller* rather than a horror movie in an attempt to distance the film from the 80s slashers. In fact, "thriller" isn't a bad description at all: *Scream* is less brooding than the average horror film and has a quicker, more action-filled pace. It seeks to thrill more than it tries to chill, if you get my drift.

Scream also brings to the table an emphasized mystery plot. It's certainly not the first to do so, but *Scream* brings its *whodunit* aspect to the forefront by having its characters spend the majority of their time—when not running from the killer—trying to figure out whom among them is the villain behind the mask. Undoubtedly the biggest anticipation audiences have before and during a *Scream* movie is trying to guess *"who's the killer?"* One of the first words you'll hear when someone describes *Scream* is *"fun,"* and both the mystery and thriller aspects are reasons why.

And yet, as apt as it is, even the "mystery thriller" label doesn't quite capture the essence of what *Scream*'s about. You hear "mystery thriller" and thoughts of private eyes and FBI agents probably come to mind before teens and masked killers do. What's more, *Scream* rarely gives out any tangible clues to the killer's identity. There are usually subtle hints as to the villain's motivation and his or her ties to the movie's overall themes, but this isn't a movie where you'll be able to think, "A-ha! Randy was wearing the same boots the other night, so his alibi doesn't cut it. I've figured it all out!" For better or worse, the reveals at the end of the *Scream* movies tend to come out of left field and pull every trick in the cinematic handbook to misdirect the audience.

Moreover, "mystery thriller" downplays the horror of *Scream* a little too much. While these movies are rarely gross-out with the gore, they are vicious, bloody and at times shocking. The suspense scenes are intense and prolonged, and while *Scream* isn't going for the creeping fear of, say, *Halloween*, it is undoubtedly trying to scare the audience with its tension. *Scream* is a horror movie.

"It's a dark comedy."

A cousin to "It's a parody," the claims of *Scream* being a dark comedy seem both apt and problematic at the same time. Dark comedy seeks to make light of a serious subject, and there are plenty of times that *Scream* does just that: after all, it's a movie in which people die in brutal knife stabbings that purports to be *fun*.

But for every ridiculous death like Tatum getting crushed in a mechanical garage door's pet opening, there are at least four that are gruesome, terrifying, or heartbreaking. You're not supposed to laugh as Casey Becker is found hanging from a tree or as Maureen Evans is stabbed in a movie theater (in fact, this moment is meant to shame the viewer for laughing at poor Maureen earlier in the scene, but more on that later). If anything, *Scream* takes joy in punishing its characters that don't take the threat seriously enough.

As breezy as many of its scenes go, where it really matters *Scream* is a deadly serious movie; note that each one ends with the survivors disquieted by the events. Even when optimistic, such as in *Scream 2* and *Scream 3*, the characters and the audience aren't laughing at the end.

Someone can make a case for *Scream* being a dark comedy, but I don't think it quite clears the bar for that title, and in any case it's an inadequate description at best.

"So what is it all about, anyway?"

I've found that the single most succinct, complete statement of the *Scream* concept is thus:

Scream *is a horror movie that takes place in the real world.*

It might take some explaining to fully make sense of that statement (that's what this book is for, in fact), but it is undoubtedly true. That's not all, though. As a "horror movie that takes place in the real world," and as such a "horror movie about horror movies," it inevitably has two other related, all-encompassing themes:

Scream *is about media, art and messages.*

And:

Scream *is about sex.*

The Disrupted Deconstruction

Let's say you get a call one night, and on the other line is a menacing voice that taunts you with mind games and threats of brutal violence. Just when you start to realize this isn't a joke, he bursts through the window in a Halloween costume, brandishes a knife, and proceeds to chase after you relentlessly.

Your first thought in this scenario would probably be something like, "*Aaaaaauuugyhh!*" Your *second* thought, though, would probably be something along the lines of, "This is unreal! It's like I'm inside of a *horror movie* or something!" And with that thought, you've already hit pretty close to the heart of *Scream*.

I'm sure the chances that any reader of this book being unfamiliar with the slasher movies of the 70s and 80s are slim to none, but it's important to establish the context into which *Scream* was released. The slasher subgenre of horror was born when genre trailblazers *Black Christmas* (1974), *Halloween* (1978), *Friday the 13th* (1980) and others (themselves taking a page from *Psycho* (1968) and the Italian horror films of the 70s) ignited an army of imitators and forged into stone what would become long-standing genre tropes, including but certainly not limited to:

- The usually silent, indestructible killer with a trademark look, often a costume or mask.
- Victims, usually teenagers, being killed while engaging in societal and moral transgressions: namely sex and drugs.
- The Final Girl: the chaste, modest protagonist who finally defeats the killer.

By the time the 90s rolled around, the slasher film—as well as the horror genre itself—was waning, not only because people got tired of seeing the same formula rehashed over and over again, but also because they no longer resembled reality. *"What's wrong with these people?"* disgruntled viewers would say about the bumbling victims on-screen, *"Why is she going outside to investigate a strange noise when her best friend was just killed the other night? Why are they splitting up? And why, oh why are they assuming the killer is dead? Haven't these people seen a horror movie before?"*

It turns out, in rehashing the same genre tropes *ad nasueum* for over a decade, slasher movies lost their power not only because of repetition or shoddy production quality, but also because they no longer resembled the real world and provided a buffer between the audience and the film. The killers were essentially fantasy monsters in the guise of a human serial killer (Michael Myers is referred to as "the bogeyman" in *Halloween*; Freddy Krueger of *A Nightmare on Elm Street* is a *literal* example) and after 1991's *The Silence of the Lambs*—a horror movie in all but pedigree—introduced terrifying humans much closer to actual serial killers, the slashers couldn't help but look absurd in comparison.

Perhaps most preposterous of all, though, was that horror movies began taking place in a world where the slasher film subgenre itself didn't seem to exist. Slasher movies had become a staple of popular culture, one where most any movie fan was familiar with how they work; anyone, that is, except the characters in a slasher film. You could forgive Laurie Strode for not being prepared for Michael Myers, but ten years later the residents of Haddonfield should know better. Haven't they seen a horror movie before? There's a million of them, how could they not know what stupid mistakes to avoid? We can only conclude that in fact, no, these characters *haven't* seen a slasher film, and moreover since they don't seem to be familiar with slasher movie clichés *at all* and are seemingly oblivious to the fact that they're breaking all kinds of movie "rules" for survival, we can only conclude that the slasher movie phenomenon as we know it simply doesn't exist in their world, and so these characters are doomed by their own ignorance.

The audience at this point had less to fear from the slasher movie because it became too obvious that the movies didn't took place in the real world; they existed in a fantasy world that "could never happen to me." People stopped taking slasher movies seriously. Budgets and studio support dropped, talented filmmakers stayed away from the genre, and the resulting schlock that was produced started getting consigned to the direct-to-video bin, a grave where it seemed the slasher movie would finally be buried forever, and it threatened to take all of the horror genre along with it.

Enter *Scream*. In its very first scene, Casey Becker (in what's become a landmark performance for Drew Barrymore) is about to watch a slasher movie on tape, is later scolded by the killer for shouting "who's there," and is even mockingly asked if she even *watches* horror movies considering all the supposed "don't do's" that she's committing.

This opening scene goes even further: before she realizes who she's on the phone with, Casey chats with the killer about other horror movies and, rather than go for generic made-up titles for the movie, straight-up name-drops *Halloween* and *A Nightmare on Elm Street* as well as Michael Myers and Freddy Krueger. Even after the killer makes his threat known, he quizzes Casey on horror movie trivia with her survival at stake.

This pre-credits scene (scratch that, actually; *Scream* has no opening credit sequence) makes the concept of the movie plain: this movie takes place in the real world as we knew it in 1996. These characters have seen horror movies and think they know what to expect; and what's more, *the killer* does as well.

The scene goes beyond the movie references to establish this, in fact: the scene extends past the death of Casey (where many horror movie opening scenes may end) and lets the audience see Mr. and Mrs. Becker's horror and anguish at discovering their daughter's murder. While the melodrama is played up just enough to keep this the film firmly in the realm of horror, *Scream* establishes early on that there are real-world traumatic consequences to the murders it showcases. These are "real" people.

Even the casting of Drew Barrymore underlines this. Being the movie's biggest star (having her face consume the entire poster didn't hurt, either), audiences naturally assumed she would be the protagonist. Having Casey (and Barrymore) be the first on the chopping block was not only a surprise, but another element of realism: no one here is a "star" unless the killer, who's premeditating these murders, considers her to be.

There's a word for this kind of thing: *deconstruction*. A piece of work that takes a genre and allows its established tropes to extend to their natural conclusions in "the real world" is "deconstructing" said genre. The presented real-world results of these tropes usually are a form of criticism, or at least a way of showing how the ideals of the genre are unworkable or unattainable in real life. The key to the deconstruction, as opposed to a parody, is that the tropes are played straight rather than for laughs. Think *Watchmen* or

The Incredibles in regards to comic books: both feature superheroes reigned in and exploited by politics and their own issues. Another example: *Unforgiven* examines the bitter later life of the type of celebrated cowboy criminal Clint Eastwood used to chew into in his salad days. Similarly, decades earlier *The Wild Bunch* explored the dark results of the western antihero that was romanticized by the film's contemporaries. In its own way, *Scream* applies a real-world treatment to the slasher flick.

Wes Craven had taken a stab at meta-horror once before. *New Nightmare* (1994) featured Freddy Krueger entering the Real World, who then went on to stalk the cast and crew of the original *A Nightmare on Elm Street*, including Craven himself. Freddy, it turns out, is an evil force of nature that was contained in the *Elm Street* movies, but when the movie series reached its end, Freddy was free to do his evil bidding on reality.

New Nightmare serves as a prototype to *Scream*. The difference, though, is that while *New Nightmare* does advocate horror movies as an outlet for the dark side of human nature, it never really dissects the nature of horror movies themselves or what they mean. *New Nightmare* is referential but doesn't quite have the introspection required to become a genre deconstruction.

So that finally settles it then, after a chapter and a half of trying to peg this movie down: *Scream* is a genre deconstruction of horror movies.

...right?

Some like to argue against this, on the grounds that *Scream* is too much a straight slasher film in and of itself to provide the necessary insight a proper deconstruction demands. Personally, I say the first *Scream*, at least, certainly qualifies, as its entire reason for being is to magnify a particular genre trait and criticize it. As the series goes on, however, something strange happens: the Real World of *Scream* slowly gets corrupted and twisted in interesting ways. The deconstruction of *Scream* gets disrupted.

Sex and the Final Girl

In one of *Scream*'s most celebrated scenes, movie geek Randy (Jamie Kennedy) presents to an obnoxious crowd of partygoers the "rules" a character must follow to survive a slasher flick. They are, as paraphrased:

+ *Don't ever have sex.*
+ *Don't ever drink or get high on drugs.*
+ *Don't ever say the words, "I'll be right back."*

Randy's right. What he doesn't get around to in his monologue, though, is examining the type of character that embodies these traits and who gets to defeat the killer at the end: the Final Girl.

"The Final Girl" is a trope most famously observed by Carol J. Clover in her 1992 book *Men, Women, and Chainsaws: Gender in the Modern Horror Film*, in which she coined the term itself. In a nutshell, Clover postulated that the Final Girl embodied a kind of purity necessary to defeat the evil embodied by the killer, and that, while the audience goes through much of the film mostly through the perspective of the killer, by the climax their identification shifts to the Final Girl's perspective as she takes up a few masculine features (such as wielding a phallic-shaped weapon) in her attempt to survive the killer.

Halloween, having cemented so many slasher genre conventions, also gets to claim the quintessential Final Girl: Laurie Strode, played by Jamie Lee Curtis in her breakthrough role. While her two friends are ditching the children they should be watching and hooking up with guys and drinking beer, Laurie takes her responsibility as a babysitter seriously, is demonstrably smart, never drinks, and is notably shy around boys (it's not a stretch at all to assume she's a virgin). Her friends all fall prey to psycho Michael Myers, but Laurie manages to evade, hide from, and fight back against him—the only reason she even has to be saved by

Dr. Loomis at the end is because, this being the first major slasher flick, Laurie doesn't know not to turn her back on a masked killer she assumes is dead.

It's fitting, then, that *Halloween* is playing on the background TV during Randy's "rules" scene, and it's no coincidence that Laurie Strode herself is the catalyst (Randy starts explaining about "the rules" in response to horny party host Stu's impatience at not having seen Jamie Lee Curtis's breasts in the movie).

Scream, of course, presents its own Final Girl: Sidney Prescott, played by Neve Campbell. As the series goes on, Sidney arguably becomes *the ultimate* Final Girl as she lives through four (!) *Scream* movies and victoriously destroys the killer each time. Sid (it's common for a Final Girl to have an androgynous-sounding name or nickname) is both a suitable example and subversion of the Final Girl trope: she's vulnerable but not mousy; she's emotional and frightened, but she never freaks out the way Alice does in *Friday the 13th* or even Laurie does at one point in *Halloween*; she starts out wary and avoidant about sex, but—in *Scream*'s most famous genre subversion—she ultimately does have sex (with the killer!) and lives to see three *Scream* sequels anyway.

The theme of sex is at the heart of *Scream*. The major background plot of the movie concerns Sidney's late mother Maureen Prescott, who was brutally murdered a year before the film starts. Sidney steadfastly believes a man named Cotton Weary killed and raped her mother, and her testimony in court has put Cotton on death row. However, Cotton's innocence is championed by tabloid TV reporter Gale Weathers, who is writing a book about Maureen's murder maintaining that Sidney's mother merely had sex with Cotton, who was subsequently framed for her murder by the true killer, whoever that may be.

It's obvious that Sidney's angered by Gale's theory (Sid clocks her in the face in one scene), and it's not hard to assume that it's not only because Gale's siding with the man she believes killed her mother, but because she's sensationalizing and exploiting her mother's death for fame and profit (Courteney Cox portrays Gale as a narcissistic opportunist). But after Casey Becker's murder and Sid's own attack by the masked killer, even Gale notices that Sid's harsh, angry insistence on Cotton Weary's guilt might be overcompensating for something: Sid herself is not even 100% sure anymore about her mother's killer, Gale realizes, even if she doesn't admit it.

We soon find out what she's compensating for: Sid eavesdrops on a couple of catty high school teens (ostensible teens, at least; the actresses look like they're pushing thirty) gossiping about the recent murders and the attack on Sidney. One of the girls accuses Sid of making up the attack for attention and even speculates that Sid herself might be the killer, going after Casey and her boyfriend in a jealous rage. Why? Because, she says, maybe Sidney is a slut—like her mother was.

It turns out Maureen Prescott had quite the reputation. The town of Woodsboro is fairly small and word gets around quick: even Sidney's friend Tatum tells her about the rumors that have gone on about her mother.

Sidney's motivation, then, becomes plain; she *needs* to believe in Cotton's guilt in order to maintain her mother's innocence. The implication is that if Maureen Prescott indeed seduced Cotton Weary and was killed by someone else, then she would have "deserved it." But if Maureen was raped by Cotton, Sidney reasons, then Maureen wasn't asking for it; her death wouldn't be her getting what was coming to her.

Maureen Prescott's death is an ironic inversion of the slut-shaming stigma for many rape victims, a phenomenon that has some victims of rape not coming forward in order to avoid untoward speculation into their private lives: if you've had too many one night stands or dressed too provocatively in the past you risk being labeled "asked for it." Sidney insists her mother *has* been raped in order to mitigate a similar judgment for her murder.

Sidney herself remains chaste, much to the chagrin of her boyfriend Billy Loomis (Skeet Ulrich, channeling a young Johnny Depp from Craven's own *A Nightmare on Elm Street*). From his first scene, Billy pressures Sidney to have sex with him, and she refuses because (a) Billy's probably coming on too strong in the first place, and (b) because she doesn't want to end up with a reputation—or fate—like that of her mother's.

After Sidney's first attack by the killer, she accuses Billy of being the culprit (all because he was on the scene with a cell phone, a nice little time capsule that we'll examine a bit later). After the police release Billy after not having any evidence on him, he lays the guilt trip on Sid, saying she'd rather accuse him of murder than make love to him.

Sidney begins to come around. She needs to lighten up, she reasons, to start getting over her mother's death and not let it get in the way of her sex life. In spite of Tatum (a spunky Rose McGowan at her best) insisting there's nothing wrong with her apprehension against having sex with Billy, Sid feels like she owes Billy for both accusing him and for stringing him along for the length of their relationship.

So, the night of Stu's party, Sidney finally relents, and she and Billy have sex in a somewhat cold scene in which we don't get the impression she really enjoys the sex too much. This isn't an act of passion on Sidney's part, it's an act of obligation, of submission—and she's just broken the first rule of the Final Girl. Randy would consider her a dead girl walking.

Fast forward to the end: we find out Billy is indeed the killer, and he reveals to Sidney that he killed her mother as well, point-blank because she was a slut, the home wrecker of his parents' marriage. And now that Sidney has had sex with him, Billy's free to kill her, too.

The ensuing climax becomes a fight for Sidney's right to her sexuality, her right to have sex—and on her terms. When she eventually triumphs over Billy, Sidney restores her mother's innocence: Maureen Prescott's crime was not that she had sex, but that she wasn't honest with her husband about her issues (we never *do* hear what Neil Prescott has to say about her affairs, and Billy's biases show in that he doesn't seem to place any blame on his own father for the breakup of their family), and in either case, it was not something she deserved to die over.

Billy's Reel Life and the Battle of the Sexes

*"At core, men are afraid women will laugh at them.
At core, women are afraid men will kill them."*

Gavin de Becker

Horror movies have traditionally been thought of as a male-oriented genre. The voyeurism, the bimbos, the macabre, the violence and gore, it's all been considered in the domain of male interests. Even in Carol J. Clover's assessment of the Final Girl largely she assumed the audience for a slasher film was mostly men: she spoke of audience identification being fluid among gender lines and how male audience members "transfer" their identification to the female protagonist's point of view at the end. For decades it was a basic, unchallenged assumption that the horror movie was a man's movie.

This isn't the case anymore, and *Scream* played a pivotal part in this re-assessment of the horror film and its audience. Women, in fact, love horror films. It's a common practice, for instance, for teenage and preteen girls to get together and rent a bunch of horror movies for marathon slumber party viewings, and it's long been observed that horror movies often make great date flicks.

It'd be easy to dismiss the assumption of male ownership of the horror genre as a product of a time of more rigid thought on gender roles, but there was another factor that turned up in the 80s: the idea that horror movies—and the slasher formula in particular—were misogynist. While this wasn't an entirely fair assertion to make against a whole genre of film—Clover's book was actually, in part, a defense of the genre against such accusations—it wasn't without merit. Many, if not most, slasher movies featured extended, voyeuristic stalking scenes in which the female victims, usually peculiarly attractive, were portrayed as promiscuous bimbos who usually got undressed or had sex. Since so many horror movies frame such scenes as if from the killer's eyes (often literally), it's not a stretch to feel like the movie invites the audience to become peeping toms.

As the 80s went on and slasher film after slasher film repeated the same tropes over again—every character that has sex gets murdered, the chaste or virginal girl survives—it became apparent to various critical and audience circles that these horror movies were advocating the punishment of those that had sex; or at least that they deserved whatever was coming to them, even the gruesome death from the hands of a masked serial killer. This interpretation of the 80s slasher movie has lived into the 21st century, where even an *A.V. Club* article about horror movie politics cited the genre as exhibiting an extremist form of socially conservative moral values.

Most any slasher film from the time period would seem to conform to this convention, but the most famous example is likely the original *Friday the 13th* from 1980. Horror fans will remember what Casey Becker unfortunately did not: the killer in this movie turned out to be Mrs. Voorhees rather than what would become the series' famous villain, Jason. Mrs. Voorhees is, in fact, Jason's mother, and she's gone mad with a vengeance at the camp counselors who were too busy having sex to notice that then-child Jason was drowning in the camp lake (it's never made clear how Jason survived "drowning" in order to eventually emerge as the grown-up psycho seen in the sequels). She's held a murderous grudge against any and all counselors at Camp Crystal Lake ever since, even those that had nothing to do with the incident.

It would be easy to discount the idea that Mrs. Voorhees's victims "deserved it" because she's the bad guy, and the bad guy is rarely right. But the fact that the Final Girl in *Friday the 13th*, Alice, is a demure, chaste, intellectual girl when compared to her fellow camp counselors arguably creates a scenario where the only reason Mrs. Voorhees is stopped is that she finally went after somebody that didn't deserve it. It winds up reinforcing, rather than refuting, the notion that Mrs. Voorhees is a fallen angel of justice.

In *Scream*, Billy Loomis apparently sees it that way exactly. His mother left their family upon discovering her husband was having an affair with Maureen Prescott, and a despondent Billy took solace in the horror movies he was a fan of—movies in which women who have sex get killed in messy ways, movies in which, from Billy's point of view, sluts get what they deserve. So, in a bid to capture that brand of movie-justice in real life, Billy recruits friend Stu Macher and proceeds to emulate the slasher movies he loves, first by killing Maureen Prescott, and then a year later, their bloodlust having not been satiated, by killing anyone they feel has wronged them in some way (most of the victims were likely of Stu's choosing: Casey Becker was an ex-girlfriend who dumped him, Principal Himbry despised wise-cracking teens such as Stu, and Tatum was his girlfriend, and as Randy quips, there's always a "bullshit" excuse to kill your girlfriend).

It's important to understand that when we watch any of the *Scream* movies, we are essentially watching two movies at once: the movie proper and the "movie" the killer is trying to create. The world of *Scream*, when it starts out, is identical to our own, the Real World of 1996, with the only exception being the existence of the town of Woodsboro and its citizens, including all the characters we get to know. The killer in each film is trying to alter the Real World into a movie universe, one that has "rules" that conform to the killer's sense of justice. In the first *Scream*, Billy is trying to turn reality into a horror movie.

Billy says this outright when he and Sidney are talking in Stu's parents' room. Sidney speaks of the trauma of her mother's death, and when Billy compares her plight to Jodie Foster's Clarice Starling of *The Silence of the Lambs*, Sid responds that life isn't a movie. Billy tells her that life, in fact, *is* a movie. Sidney doesn't yet understand that he isn't speaking metaphorically.

An earlier scene is even more important because it outlines the central conflict of *Scream*: the fear that the sexes have for each other. The film abides by the old adage that men fear that women will laugh at them (read: abandonment, humiliation) while women fear that men will kill them. Billy and Sidney encounter each other in the halls of Woodsboro High School and he implores her to get over her mother's murder from a year ago. He cites that he has done so with his own mother, who had abandoned him. Sidney is rightfully appalled that Billy would suggest that their suffering is equal. It might be tough to discern upon first watch, but with this scene the lines are drawn and the battle of the sexes that keeps going until the end of *Scream 3* is officially on.

It's because of this scene that Billy must be the killer (savvy viewers might also pick up on the fact that the script's unsolicited information about Billy's past is a kind of Chekhov's Gun, a plot element introduced with just enough fanfare that it must be followed up on later in the story). When we consider the major themes of sex, adultery and horror, the only other truly plausible suspect is Sidney's father, Neil Prescott, whose motive would presumably be that Sid's relationship with Billy would signify her becoming a "slut" like the wife that cheated on him (indeed, the script makes Sid's father the only other major suspect and red herring in the film). This scene between Sid and Billy, however, puts them into direct opposition with each other: the conflict is between them, and so Billy as the culprit makes the most sense.

I'd like to take a moment to mention that both Skeet Ulrich and especially Neve Campbell are excellent in this scene, as is Wes Craven's direction. On paper, writer Kevin Williamson's signature witty dialogue reads almost preposterously catty for what should be a serious scene. Craven focuses the camera on the characters' faces and silences the score to create an intimate moment free of excess melodrama. Campbell and Ulrich read through their lines with utter conviction and minimal sass.

The only character that truly realizes what's going on is Randy, the movie geek. Randy (played by Jamie Kennedy as a Gen-X slacker smartass) recognizes that the killer isn't just trying to create the aesthetic of a horror film, but its formula as well. In the scene where he's working at the video store, Randy tells Stu and the audience exactly what's going to happen at the end: Billy is the killer, Neil Prescott is a red herring, and Billy's motivation has something to do with sex. The only thing that's slipped under his radar is that Stu is in on the murders, too.

When Billy discovers Randy and the accusations he's making, the movie gives us a look at "the killer" unmasked: Billy and Stu surround Randy and intimidate him in exactly the manner they do to Sidney at the end when they reveal themselves. Randy knows he's looking at the killer as Billy faces him, but even he doesn't understand the enormity of the situation before him: with Billy and Stu having ganged up on him, Randy is literally in the killer's grasp, and likely the only reason he's left alive in this scene is that he's in a public place.

When the climax finally reveals that "the killer" is in fact two, Billy and Stu, it's one of *Scream*'s finest moments not just because it's an admittedly sweet twist in and of itself, but also because it reveals the truth about what has transpired: throughout the film, the audience had taken for granted that they were watching a horror movie and suspended their belief accordingly (if they were a good sport, that is). The killer could appear seemingly at will and always seemed to know where the victims were. These are just Things That Happen in Horror Movies and so the audience went along with it. In fact, considering there's no explanation for the killer's distinct voice over the phone (a voice that sounded nothing like any character present) until the big reveal, for all the audience knew the killer probably had some crazy multiple personality syndrome with different voices, or perhaps the movie would pull a *Friday the 13th* and introduce an unseen new character entirely to be the killer. Maybe the killer is a nigh-indestructible quasi-superhuman like Michael Myers and will come back again and again as the star of the franchise. It's a horror movie, any outlandish thing is possible.

The third-act twist isn't just that there are two killers, but that for much of the running time *we weren't watching a horror movie as we knew it at all.* The killer's voice on the phone? An illusion created by an electronic distortion box. The killer's apparent omniscience? An illusion created by the two teens covering for each other. The entire bloody episode, in fact, was an illusion created by Billy and Stu, even though it had real consequences. We weren't watching a horror movie, we were watching two guys try to turn the Real World *into* a horror movie, and as they explain to Sidney, they've already got the ending planned: they're going to frame her father, Neil Prescott, so in this movie they're creating *he* is the killer.

One of Billy and Stu's fatal mistakes is that they buy the illusion themselves. Billy spends most of the movie trying to bed Sidney, and while the audience probably assumes Billy is a horny teen like any other, it turns out Billy wants to take Sidney's virginity so badly because *he wants to kill her*—the horror movie rules say that the chaste Final Girl can defeat the killer, so he must take that out of the equation. Notice that when the killer first attacks Sidney, there's a moment when he pins her down and has a clear moment to stab her, but he toys with her instead, taking up just enough time for her to escape—right into Billy's comforting arms. It's all manipulation so he can have sex with her and subsequently kill her. But in the end, Billy and Stu's plans are undone because unlike a genre movie, the Real World has no rules.

The ending of *Scream* plays out like no other slasher film before it—even the aforementioned *Friday the 13th* still more or less climaxes like a standard slasher despite having an unexpected middle-aged woman as the antagonist. In *Scream*, there is no final chase scene involving the costumed killer; *Scream* at this point has already had more chase scenes than some 80s slasher films put together. *Scream*'s last reel steps outside of the horror movie framework (again, we're not watching a "movie") and consists mostly of stand-offs with a gun (!) and plot twist after plot twist followed by a couple of good ol' knock-down drag-out fights.

Billy and Stu's illusion falls apart on them. Victims they've left for dead come back alive and kicking: Gale, Randy, and eventually Dewey. The rules for survival all get broken: Randy gets piss drunk and survives, Sidney has sex and survives, Gale says "I'll be right back," and survives. And the horror movie-inspired justice Billy craves eludes him when the "slut" Sidney jams her fingers into his stab wound—a kind of payback rape—before he is blown away from gunfire by Gale. And although he provides one last jump scare, Sidney provides another bullet through his head that destroys him for good. The film fades to black with Gale Weathers recording her news report—a nonfiction reality being presented in contrast to Billy and Stu's fictional fantasy—against the sun rising, with no sign of a "the evil is still *out there!*" coda that's a staple of the genre. Reality has prevailed—and so has Sidney's argument.

Some critics have accused *Scream* of being hypocritical: a horror movie that agrees that horror movies are harmful and advocate deplorable violence. Lyz Kingsley of *And You Call Yourself a Scientist* made the argument that because its villains are youths imitating horror films, that *Scream* is ultimately blaming horror films for real-life violence. What's more, Kingsley says, the movie's empathy for the female perspective is undone by the blame it places on Maureen Prescott for the murders.

These criticisms are off-base. *Scream* doesn't "blame the movies" for violence and misogyny; rather, it is a refutation of the weak defense some genre filmmakers and fans had provided for the genre, which was that it was merely low-brow fantasy that didn't aspire to the moral pretensions critics would find in it. In layman's terms, *"It's just a stupid movie, stop reading so much into it."*

Scream takes issue with that, because that reasoning devalues horror's own value as a piece of work, and it's this very devaluing that helped lead to the general drop in quality of horror films by the dawn of the 90s that drove the audience away. *Scream*'s argument is that *the message the receiver hears is more important than the one the messenger intends.* Horror filmmakers never intended to make films that advocate for violence and misogyny, but if that's what the audience is getting out of it (and if what's on screen follows for such an interpretation), the answer is to rise to the challenge, not shrink from it. Instead of purposely aiming to be a "bad movie" in order to keep the formula going, *Scream* aims to be a good movie that's at least about something, regardless if one agrees that it succeeds or not. *Scream* doesn't hate horror movies. On the contrary, *Scream* loves them and wants to inspire the genre to be something more. Think horror films advocate violence and archaic sexual politics? *Scream* responds: try this one.

As for Lyz Kingsley's charge that *Scream* blames the murders on Maureen Prescott and in effect "blames the victim" just as Billy Loomis does, I'll say that if she needed the movie to be transparent enough to have a big redemption scene for Maureen in which we see or hear Sidney pontificate on women's right to have sex, I'll admit we don't get that. But the self-evidence of *Scream*'s rejection of Billy's values—by having Sidney destroy him in the face of his manipulation in taking her virginity—will be enough for the rest of us.

Scream, in fact, is arguably the woman's slasher film; one that's about the female sexual experience (in fact, if anything, the *Scream* series has a bit of a misandrist streak, but more on that in a bit). In yet another example of its seminal nature, *Scream* spearheaded a movement in horror to capture female audiences, and in the coming years *The Ring*, *Paranormal Activity*, *P2*, and *Buffy the Vampire Slayer* on TV would court women as well. *Scream* reminded people—and Hollywood—that horror wasn't just a man's game.

A Ghostface in the Machine

Every film is a product of its time, and *Scream* is no different. It's a movie that could have only ever been made in the mid to late 90s. One reason for that, as mentioned earlier, is because of the specific state of the horror film genre at the time. There's one major aspect of *Scream*, though, that's been a little underappreciated, and it has everything to do with when it debuted: *Scream* was the first horror film of the information age.

Scream is hardly the first horror film to have its menace antagonizing victims over the phone, but never before was the threat being made over the receiver so immediate. *Black Christmas* (1974) and *When a Stranger Calls* (1979) both famously featured scenes in which the psycho called up to torment his victims. Being the 70s, however, these calls were all being made on landline phones, so the potential in telephone stalking scenes wasn't exactly abundant. You could be reasonably sure the killer wasn't nearby while he was on the phone (in *When A Stranger Calls*, it is in fact a Shocking Plot Twist that the killer was calling from an extension within the same house), and the killer had to be tied to the phone while he was making these calls, anyhow. If a horror movie featured the killer deploying phone calls to potential victims, it was usually as an initial "they're being stalked" scene, and the calls were often just the killer breathing heavily into the receiver or something equally unintelligible.

Something interesting happened between the end of the 80s and the time *Scream* stabbed its way into theaters in December 1996: the cellular phone had become cheap and plentiful enough that a slasher villain's M.O. could be plausibly based almost entirely on its use. And use it the movie did. No longer was the killer simply calling from afar from a fixed position to breathe heavily into the phone or leave some obscene message. Now, the killer is calling you up to tell you that he's standing outside your front porch and that *he's watching you right now*. Oh, and if you don't answer his questions correctly he's going to gut you like a fish.

Urban legends are often formed with the intent of revealing the dark side of new, supposedly helpful facets of daily life: when the microwave debuted, for instance, rumors swirled at how often they would spontaneously explode or melt your kitchen with radiation. *Scream*, too, exploits a natural fear in supposed innovations to our way of life. Cell phones can be ridiculously convenient and even life savers. A plethora of subsequent horror movies, in fact, have bent over backwards to find excuses for their characters to somehow lose their phones or be out of signal to rule out an easy escape. *Scream* got in on the ground floor with the cell phone, warning us that it can be an instrument of danger just as much as it can be a tool for aid.

The world wide web itself doesn't make an appearance in the first *Scream*, but its presence is approximated with Sidney's use of "DeafTyper," a program on her computer that performs the function of a TTY machine. Sidney presumably uses it to chat with a deaf pen pal, but for all we know she could also be using it as an impromptu instant messenger, silently "talking" with her friends about any subject she pleases without her father being able to overhear. Even when Sidney uses DeafTyper as a last-ditch effort to contact 911 when the killer has invaded her home, the operator would assume that the person on the other line is deaf, and of course Sidney isn't.

Scream posits that the new media of cell phones and the web are still like the media that came before: they're a filter that reality has to pass through, and whatever comes out the other end, however close, isn't quite the same as actual reality. Sidney isn't deaf like the operator on the other side of the TTY machine would presume; and when she's typing in her room in her first scene, she isn't working on a report for school like her father might think (and the audience might think, too: in the mid 90s the sound of typing was still synonymous with work), she's actually chatting with her friends. In the same vein, the killer uses the cell phone as a tool to facilitate his horror movie fantasy.

An older form of mass media has a major presence in *Scream*, as well: the television. The TV is all over *Scream* and presents the movie's duality: it's often in the background blaring news reports (and plot exposition) as well as the horror movies the characters watch throughout the film.

The news reports represent the nonfictional, "real" side of *Scream*, but that reality is undermined by the journalists' lust for scandal and sensation: it puts the tragedy of the killings in Woodsboro into a different context, one in which murder becomes melodramatic and even fun. The teens of *Scream*, having lived most of their lives in such a culture, thus display a somewhat dulled and indifferent attitude to the murders happening around them, and in some extreme cases, a downright cruel one: a pair of kids run around the halls of the school dressed in the killer's costume and one even scares Sidney in the restroom (viewers often mistake this for the actual killer, but the costumed man in this scene does not carry a weapon, his loud grunts are completely out of the killer's M.O., and he sounds nothing like either Billy or Stu; the scene is deliberately confusing to underline Sidney's paranoia at being stalked), and later, drunk teens excitedly drive off to catch a glimpse of Principal Himbry's corpse while the gettin's good.

This aspect of *Scream* was informed by the O.J. Simpson trial, still fresh in the public consciousness at the time of the film's release. The murder case became a circus and a national cultural sensation, becoming the butt of late night talk show jokes, pithy water cooler conversation and much more. Combine that silliness with the general apathy and cynicism of young Generation X in all of its *Beavis and Butthead* glory, and Williamson's presumption of youthful 90s attitudes to murder seemed apt at the time. This presumption, however, was later proven incorrect. The Columbine School massacre of 1999 showcased that even 90s teenagers and news media could face grim tragedy and its aftermath with the utmost sincerity. It's one of the few insights of *Scream* that, in hindsight, doesn't hit the mark. Nonetheless, *Scream*'s handling of certain members of the news media *does*.

Leading the pack of journalists that have swarmed Woodsboro for a hot scoop is Gale Weathers, the tabloid reporter who champions Cotton Weary's innocence. Gale is vain, conniving and temperamental, the kind of person who realizes the possibility of saving an innocent man on death row and grins at how it will affect her book sales. It's important to note, though, that Gale is never outright evil: in the end, Gale is working to uncover the truth. She's an agent on the side of the Real World in the face of Billy and Stu's horror show. She simply does the right thing for the wrong reasons, but even though she's not above embellishing a few details (we find out that she exaggerated the gruesomeness of Kenny's death, her first camera man, in her book in *Scream 2*), as long as Gale is dedicated to exposing what's real and true, she could never be the villain and thus never be the killer.

On the other side of the coin, the TV is also home to the horror movies watched by the characters of *Scream*: the partygoers watch *Halloween*, the video store has *Frankenstein* running on their display, Billy talks about watching *The Exorcist* and how it reminds him of his relationship with Sidney. This might sound obvious, but just as the news reports on the televisions represent a harsh, underlying reality, so too do the horror films on the televisions represent Billy and Stu's vision for reshaping their lives.

Wes Craven made sure that the TV shown in the background at Casey Becker's house at the start of the movie display the solid blue screen of a TV on a blank input channel, because audiences at the time had grown accustomed to their own TVs and the blank, blue screens that appeared while loading a tape into the VCR. The blue TV screen behind Casey is not just there because her movie was about to start, but it's a reference to how *Billy and Stu's* "movie" is starting as well.

Similarly, at the climax Sidney kills Stu by crushing and electrocuting his head with a TV, which, of course, was playing a horror movie. It's a visual capsule of what's happening in the scene: the horror fantasy collapsing on the killer who started it, and as the killer is destroyed, the TV and the horror flick are destroyed along with it. Just as Casey's blue TV screen means the horror is about to start, the destruction of the TV on Stu's head means the horror is about to end.

And when *Scream* does end, it cements itself as a time capsule for that short period at the dawn of the new media age, capturing the fears of a society as it stepped into a new century, one where even interconnectedness and self-awareness may still not be enough to save you.

Part II—
SCREAM 2

A Stab in the Black

It's the aim of every *Scream* villain to turn reality into a horror movie. At the end of the original *Scream*, though, Billy and Stu's violent fantasy came crashing down on them as the real world refused to bend to any of their movie world's rules, and they were destroyed along with it. As the movie closed, it would seem that the killers' attempt to alter reality had completely failed. Except as *Scream 2* opens we find that, in a small but significant way, they *didn't*.

As mentioned earlier, at the beginning of *Scream* its world is identical to our own with the exception of the fictional town of Woodsboro and our cast of characters. When *Scream 2* begins, there's an additional difference: in real life, the movie *Scream* exists and became a pop-culture phenomenon.

Yet the *Scream* universe *does* find a way to insert itself into... itself. When the Dimension Films logo fades to black and *Scream 2* starts, we find a young couple in line outside of a theater to see a horror movie. As the scene unfolds we discover that the horror movie they're watching is a dramatization of the events that happened in the original *Scream*. So it appears that the universe of *Scream* has indeed found a way to reconcile with our actual reality.

Except as the first scene of this film being watched by the characters commences, things look different right off the bat. Casey Becker's decked out in a bathrobe and is about to take a shower when the killer calls, and she looks thinner, and her house has a glass ceiling, and that dialogue she has with the killer sure sounds a lot more tacky and forced, doesn't it?

This isn't *Scream* they're watching. It's *Stab*, a schlocky, poor-man's version of *Scream*, its script having been adapted from *The Woodsboro Murders*, Gale Weather's bestselling book that recounts the harrowing murder spree by Billy and Stu. Gale wrote the book presumably based on her own recollection of the events of *Scream* as well as interviews with other survivors and law enforcement. This book was then interpreted into a written script by a screenwriter, and then this script was, in turn, interpreted and visualized by a film director. Like that classic game of 'telephone,' the fidelity of reality is repeatedly diminished as it goes through so many filters, and in *Stab* we see the end result. It's the first major evidence that what Billy and Stu had wrought in *Scream* actually *has* had an effect on their universe.

The second major piece of evidence, of course, is that they've inspired a *sequel*: another killer is on the loose, and the young couple of college kids we open with are lined up as the first victims.

The pair is Maureen Evans (Jada Pinkett in her pre-Mrs. Smith days) and Phil Stevens (Omar Epps in one of his first major roles). They're on a date and Phil has managed to acquire tickets to an advanced screening of *Stab*. Pinkett plays Maureen (not to be confused with Sidney's late mother Maureen Prescott; more on that later) as a Sassy Black Girl, but although she's stereotypical she stops just short of being a caricature: she's feisty and demanding but not dumb or mean. Phil is patient with her but has a slight "the things I put up with for women" attitude in regards to her (it's not readily apparent how long they've been together; there's a first-or-second date vibe to the scene but they act like they know each other pretty well).

While in line for *Stab*, Maureen complains to Phil about his taking her to see a slasher movie. According to her, slashers are "dumbass" movies for white people, and she pontificates on the lackluster black representation in the horror genre. While even Phil rolls his eyes at her, she does have a point: even more than other genres, horror has been almost exclusively the domain of white people. There have been black actions stars, black drama stars... but black *horror* stars? Black characters (or any minority, really) are still a rarity in horror movies, and when they do show up it tends to be in either exploitation fare (*Blacula* and *Leprechaun in the Hood*, anyone?) or they're in token cannon fodder roles. It must have taken Kevin Williamson an astronomical amount of willpower to resist having Maureen proclaim, "I bet you anything a black girl dies first." It would be obscene, though, not to point out a notable exception: *Night of the Living Dead* (1968) not only has a black protagonist, Ben, but the film treats him with a refreshing casualness; the movie never mentions race outright.

Scream 2 suddenly has a total of *four* black characters after its predecessor had an all-white cast (I think even all of the *extras* were white). The first two victims being black is an obvious contrivance: the killer is trying to create a horror sequel and one of the unspoken rules of horror sequels is that token minorities start showing up (even *Scream 2* doesn't say this out loud). The other two black characters, though, *aren't* contrivances: we might expect Hallie (Elise Neal) and Joel (Duane Martin) to have plot-armor because it would just be too mean to kill off *every* black character, or perhaps because the movie wants to atone for savagely killing off its first black characters in the beginning of the movie, or *perhaps* one or both of them is the killer because, hey, even Randy says that would be a neat little twist.

However, though the *Scream* world is slowly turning into a movie universe, we're not quite there yet. *Scream 2* still largely resembles reality. The two characters do not turn out to be token nor do they have plot-armor: Hallie is Sidney's closest college friend and succumbs to the killer, and Joel survives (he's the only character with the sense to get the Hell out of dodge) while helping Gale to realize she actually wants to become a nicer person. In the end, their being black had nothing to do with anything at all (it's also refreshing that Hallie and Joel have nothing to do with each other, nor do they have a connection to Maureen and Phil). *Scream 2* still takes place in a quasi-reality, and in the real world, sometimes people are just black.

As Maureen finishes her rant, she and Steve enter the building, and it's already a little remarkable that the movie so far has done absolutely nothing nominally creepy: no heavy music or ominous camera angles, none of the obvious things a horror movie usually does to build tension... except it still kind of *is* tense, isn't it? It's Hitchcock's famous observation in action: a seemingly normal scene of people having dinner can be made into a harrowingly suspenseful scene without any changes, just the knowledge that there's a ticking time bomb underneath the dinner table. So it is with *Scream 2*: the audience knows going into a movie called "Scream" that it's a horror movie, and anyone who's seen the first knows that there's a serial killer on the prowl, and everyone knows that something bad is going to happen in the first scene of a horror movie. Opening the movie on such a nonchalant note in a *very* public setting isn't fooling anyone, nor is *Scream 2* trying to: the audience knows something *has* to happen, and the scene has its own kind of teasing tension because we're not sure *when* or *how* it's going to happen. It's like a jack in the box, only this time the box is invisible.

Scream 2 continues its tease as ushers hand out *Stab* brand costumes identical to what the killer wears, introducing a way the killer could be present in costume while still remaining hidden. Finally, the audience knows Shit's About To Go Down when Maureen and Phil: (a) split up; and (b) the movie follows Phil into the restroom—we know a movie isn't going to show a character going to the bathroom for no reason (and the restroom's about the only place you could relatively isolate a character in this setting, as well).

When the proverbial jack finally jumps out of its box, the killer demonstrates his newfound flexibility in the disrupted reality of *Scream*: he kills Phil by stabbing his head through a restroom stall wall, an action that's wildly implausible but makes a kind of dream-logic movie sense when you see it on screen (the killer is able to do more improbable things as *Scream 2* goes on and the horror fantasy takes over). The scene is all the more surprising because it doesn't pull the expected "the killer will be one of the moviegoers" card. In fact, when *Scream 2* does make this play in the build up to Maureen's kill, it's a kind of reversal: instead of the movie trying to surprise us, we *know* it's the killer when he sits down next to Maureen wearing Phil's clothing, and the movie milks the moment for all its worth.

Maureen finally gets it: the killer brandishes a knife and skewers her, and continues to do so even as she futilely tries to get away. The rowdy crowd doesn't notice because they're too busy raving as the on-screen faux-Casey Becker is getting similarly filleted. In a last, desperate bid to get everyone's attention, Maureen heads to the front of the theater and stumbles in front of the screen, the image from the projector overlaying her bloody, wounded body. Maureen lets out a blood-curling scream that finally has the crowd pausing, trying to understand the sight before them.

As much as it gleefully bathes in its own meta-horror, the *Scream* series never explicitly breaks the fourth wall, but it's interesting to think that in a subtle way it does here. While Maureen is standing in front of the screen, for a moment the camera switches to her perspective: the audience of the theater watching her, the near-blinding brightness of the projector light obscuring some of her vision. If someone from within the movie could somehow look through the screen, this view of the audience would be exactly what they would see.

The next shot faces Maureen as she sobs. Obviously she's going through a harrowing experience, but it's not a cry of terror or pain she's letting out here, it's a mournful wail, a lament at having realized the horrible truth: she in fact *is* in a horror movie, and that the reason she's dying is because a crowd of people have paid money in order to be entertained by watching her get killed. In-movie, it's a pseudo hallucinatory rationalization of a dying person, but it's ironically the unvarnished truth. Maureen is the only character, including Randy, who ever understands that the presence of the killers has turned reality into a horror film, not just metaphorically, but in literal terms.

The crowd is still left dumbstruck and confused as Maureen drops dead in front of the screen. They came to *Stab* to see someone die, and they got it. Maureen was presented as an obnoxious character, and no doubt there were some viewers watching *Scream* 2 that were probably looking forward to seeing her get whacked. By emphasizing Maureen's suffering when she does get the axe, the movie subverts this desire. The end of the scene goes by pretty swiftly before the title card appears, but thoughtful viewers may find that the scene asks them to take a step back and examine why we want to see horror films. Some of us want to see people try to survive, while some of us want to see people die. If it's the latter, what does that say about us?

The Walking Question Mark

There's a horror filmmaker axiom that what you can't see is always scarier than what you *can* see. Fear is fueled by uncertainty, and people fear what they don't know or understand. People cite *Jaws* as a famous example, where the audience doesn't get to see the killer Great White shark until the end of the movie. The creature of *Alien* is legitimately terrifying even when you *do* see it, but a lot of its power is diminished in a few shots near the very end when you can see it very clearly against a white background, where it becomes apparent that the alien is just a guy in a suit.

In the opening Casey Becker sequence of the first *Scream*, it would appear that the movie was going to abide by this. You don't see who throws the chair through the glass doors, and the following couple of shots of the killer are from a distance and obscured a bit by smoke. But from the moment the masked killer catches Casey through a window (in a big close up, no less), *Scream* is not at all timid in showing him off in all his costumed glory in his every scene afterward, apparently violating the prevailing wisdom. In fact, the killer's visage appears even when he's not around, as teenage pranksters impersonate him by wearing the same costume while running throughout the school. By the beginning of *Scream 2*, we're confronted by dozens of costumed "killers" in the audience, and Phil even encounters two of them hogging the urinals in the restroom. Far from being hidden from view, the killer in *Scream* is all over the place.

The costumed figure, affectionately dubbed "Ghostface" by fans (the spelling "Ghost Face" is a trademark of Fun World, the costume company that originally made the mask used in the film) taking after Tatum in the first *Scream*, was merely referred to as a masked killer in Kevin Williamson's original script, without any detailed description. The filmmakers stumbled upon the now famous white mask when location scouting for the film, and Wes Craven liked it so much not only because it was pretty spooky looking in itself, but because it was a mask that conceivably anybody could get a hold of. The mask is often touted to have been inspired by the Edvard Munch painting "The Scream." Though the mask does bear a slight resemblance in terms of shape and expression, I'm not so sure that's actually the case (honestly, I think people largely assume this is so because of both works' respective titles). Regardless, a connection between the mask and the painting would be apt, because the Munch's art speaks to society's isolating effect on its depicted screaming man, much like how film, media, and the very costume the killer wears are isolating factors for the characters in *Scream*.

Similar to the mask, Ghostface was given a black cloak to wear because Craven wanted an outfit that would obscure the entire body of the killer, so virtually *anybody* could be wearing it. To back this up, the *Scream* series pretty much *does* let anybody wear it. Aside from the killers, the mask or costume is worn by the aforementioned pranksters at Woodsboro High, by Principal Himbry goofing around in his office, by the moviegoers (including Phil at one point) at the *Stab* screening, dozens of Ghostface costumes hang from racks in *Scream 3*, and a crowd of attendees sport the mask at Stab-a-thon in *Scream 4* (including Gale undercover). At the end of the first *Scream*, even *Sidney* dons the costume to turn the tables on Billy. Ghostface's voice, too, is replicated by innocent jokesters in *Scream 2* and *4*.

Such ubiquity is enabled by the fact that Ghostface doesn't actually exist: he's an identity created by Billy and Stu and assumed by each film's villain thereafter. Ghostface is just another creation of the fictional horror realm that the killers seek to realize. There are moments where Ghostface acts like the expected slasher villain: when not in a hurry or he has his prey cornered, Ghostface will savor the moment, slowly stepping toward his victim and making the occasional tilt or nod of the head. However, this being the Real World, Ghostface must act like the normal man that he is and not the invincible monster that the killers would have him be. It may be frighteningly easy to kill someone in real life, but probably not as easy as some slasher movies would have you believe: *maybe* a few people will be too petrified to take action, but most people have a fight-or-flight instinct and they're going to run, fight back, or resist in any way possible. Thus enables two of Ghostface's most famous characteristics: he often makes a mad dash for his victims with the tenacity of a wild animal (notice in *Scream 2* when Gale narrowly blocks his way from an open door with a shelf, he swings his knife madly through the narrow opening in frustration); and he's actually fairly clumsy for a slasher villain—in his haste he's often tripping over furniture, getting hit by random objects thrown by desperate victims, and on two occasions he actually gets knocked out cold.

The first and most famous scene in which Ghostface is unconscious is the hailed Car Scene from *Scream 2*. In it Sidney and Hallie are trapped in a crashed cop car that Ghostface had hijacked. The doors and windows having been locked (it being a police car makes it especially difficult to get out of), Sid and Hallie have no choice but to try to exit through the open driver's side window—and climb over the killer's unconscious body. The scene is *Scream*'s most blatant violation of the vaunted "less is more" approach to seeing the threat: in order to emphasize just *how close* Sid and Hallie have to get to the killer, we get extreme, loving close-ups of Ghostface's mask that engulf the screen as Sidney slowly, cautiously crawls past him. Note also that the obscuring nature of the killer's costume means Sid and Hallie can't even be 100% sure he *is* unconscious.

Scream doesn't always put Ghostface front and center: obviously we never see him while on the phone with a victim until he pops out of hiding, and especially in *Scream 2* a common sight of Ghostface is him in the background and out of focus: notably when the he sneaks in to the Omega Beta Zeta sorority house unbeknownst to Cici (Sarah Michelle Gellar) in the foreground, as well as the cat-and-mouse sequence in which Gale tries to hide and evade Ghostface in a campus recording studio. The camera follows her in the foreground, while Ghostface is continually lurking in the background: a reminder that danger lies in the periphery.

But the *Scream* movies are able to get away with chucking aside much of the prevailing wisdom of obscuring the threat because *Ghostface himself* obscures the threat. There's no need to cast the monster in shadows to make it scarier: Ghostface *is* the shadow that hides the killer in the dark. The Ghostface image isn't a character so much as a giant walking "?" with a knife. Because of this, *Scream* is still able to play on audience uncertainty and fear of the unknown, no matter how often we see the killer and how much he fills up the frame.

Derek and Mrs. Loomis: The Sexes Strike Again

Men take a lot of heat in *Scream*. They are constantly the bad guys, trying to enact a violent male power fantasy over women through serial killing sprees. Not all men are killers, but all killers are men. Notice in *Scream* how the male characters openly balk at the idea of a female killer: it takes a man to be able to gut someone like Ghostface does, they say. The entire first film in the series was basically an extended metaphorical battle of the sexes. Remember: in *Scream*, men fear that women will laugh at them, women fear men will kill them. In the first film, the woman (Sidney) comes out on top because her need for safety from violence is more important than the man's (Billy's) desire to not be rejected. *Scream 2* sets up a rematch, although not without adding a few twists and reversals of its own.

When we last left Sidney Prescott, she had just thwarted her boyfriend Billy's attempt to complete his horror movie-inspired series of murders on the anniversary of her mother's death. Billy was responsible for *that* death, too, as well as seducing Sid into having sex with him for the express purpose of being able to kill her to satisfy his slasher movie brand of sexual justice.

So it's understandable in *Scream 2* when new murders start happening a couple years later at her new school, Windsor College—murders that mimic the *modus operandi* of Billy's exactly—that she starts experiencing trust issues regarding her new boyfriend, Derek (Jerry O'Connell). Sidney tells him to keep his distance from her because she doesn't want him to possibly get hurt, but they both know that deep down, at least, her experiences have left her paranoid of even supposed loved ones.

Sadly for Derek, he's innocent and Sid can't see it. Aside from one red herring moment where his alibi sounds a little suspicious, *Scream 2* bends over backwards to show that Derek is a good guy. He's presented as a mirror-image version of Billy: where Billy exudes a dark Johnny Depp-esque cool, Derek is wholesome; where Billy sneaks into

Sidney's room and pressures her into sex, Derek is respectful of her boundaries.

Derek even gets a mirror-image version of the scene from the first *Scream* between Billy and Sidney at Woodsboro High (*Scream 2* reiterates that scene's importance by reprising it in a clip from *Stab*—and as I pointed out earlier, the slightly altered dialogue sounds ridiculous coming out of Tori Spelling and Luke Wilson in their deliberately low-rent portrayals of Sidney and Billy). Derek tries to win over Sid's trust by randomly breaking into song in the middle of the campus food court. He shamelessly butchers "I Think I Love You" in front of dozens of strangers in a cheesy but nonetheless charming serenade. What's more, he gives her a necklace with his fraternity letters, an apparent no-no that he knows will get him hazed by his frat brothers. The implication of this scene is that *Derek is not afraid of humiliation in regards to Sidney*. Unlike Billy, he does not fear rejection or being "laughed at" by women. Billy's scene proves he has to be the killer. Derek's scene proves he *cannot* be the killer.

Sidney is so affected by the murders surrounding her, though, that even after Derek's display of devotion there are moments where Sidney's trust in him falters. At the end, when

Mickey (Timothy Olyphant), one of her friends, reveals himself to be one of the killers, he's able to manipulate her uncertainty, causing her to hesitate to free a tied-up Derek (it wouldn't have mattered at least, since Mickey winds up just shooting him dead anyhow).

Mickey has his own agenda, but his partner in crime is the real brains behind their murderous operation: it turns out to be Mrs. Loomis, Billy's mother. She cites revenge as her motivation, but by picking up Billy's mantle where he left off, she's carrying the torch for *his* motivation as well. In fact, Mrs. Loomis (Laurie Metcalf chewing the scenery as if it were going to expire soon) *does* bring up Maureen Prescott's dalliance with her husband as deserving of blame for the whole bloody affair.

At first, the killer now being a 40-something year old woman would seem like a refutation of the "killer must be a man" adage of the first *Scream*. Literally it is, but in some important ways it isn't. Remember that we're watching two movies at once here: *Scream 2*, the movie proper, and the invented narrative the killer seeks to bring about. The "killer" is the Ghostface identity, which is always undeniably male, and in the end Mrs. Loomis designs to peg the murders entirely on Mickey while she rides off scot-free. Mrs. Loomis is continuing Billy's mission while assuming the Ghostface identity and planning to set Mickey up to take the fall: thematically, it all points to how in order to become a killer, Mrs. Loomis must transform into a man.

Scream 2 reflects on this (though it isn't apparent unless it's in hindsight) in its opening act: Ghostface is hiding in a stall in the men's room at the movie theater. The killer attracts Phil, who's in the adjacent stall, to press his ear up to the shared stall wall by going into some incoherent, frantic whispering. The murmurings are higher-pitched and feminine-sounding, far from the menacing, masculine growl of Ghostface over the phone. Finally, just before the killer takes the opportunity to thrust a knife through the wall and into Phil's head, two words finally become intelligible: "Listen, mommy."

Even if it's actually Mickey in the costume in this scene, this moment is the only real indicator that the killer might have a feminine side and that there is a maternal edge to the motivations this time around. The only time this whispering happens (in the entire series!) is in this one scene when the killer is held up in the stall: just as Ghostface is hiding this newfound feminine, motherly dimension inside a men's restroom, Mrs.

Loomis hides behind Billy, Mickey, and the Ghostface identity itself.

Somewhat on a tangent, of all the killers in the series, Mrs. Loomis seems the least versed in the conventions of the slasher film; it's never mentioned that she cares at all about them other than the fact that she wants to continue the murders that her son started. It's fitting, then, that the sequel she tries to produce turns out to be a *formula* sequel: one that tries to reproduce the success of the first story by simply repeating the same beats: think *Home Alone 2: Lost in New York*, *Friday the 13th Part 2*, *The Hangover II*. This is signified by the killers' targeting of victims that share the same name of those in Woodsboro (and in the same order, too)—Maureen Evans for Maureen Prescott, Phil Stevens for Steven Orth, and Casey "Cici" Cooper for Casey Becker. This pattern gets broken when the victim afterward is *Randy*, who, by insulting the name of her son to her over the phone, had enraged Mrs. Loomis into killing him out of sequence. The formula having been broken (and one of the most popular characters of the series having shockingly gotten the axe), the movie goes forward on a more unpredictable note.

In that same vein, *Scream 2* starts out as a formula sequel thematically: a reprise of the battle-of-the-sexes tale, but this time with an unpredictable turn that isn't wholly apparent until the end: each side has an advocate from the opposite sex: Derek for women and Mrs. Loomis for men.

Mickey, Cotton, and Sidney's Media Matters

One of *Scream 2*'s first scenes is a classroom discussion that includes Randy, Cici, and Mickey. The topic: the recent murders of Maureen Evans and Phil Stevens. Because they were stabbed with a knife just like the victims of the movie they came to watch (which was even called *Stab*), the students have an open debate over the culpability of film and media violence for inciting real-life violence. Randy and Cici advocate for film's innocence, while Mickey and others in the class argue for their guilt.

Although it's not as transparent, this scene is like the original *Scream*'s video store scene in that it tells us who the killer (or one of the killers, as it were) is going to be. Randy doesn't quite peg it this time—this early into the movie he's not even convinced yet that a new murder spree is underway—but he's debating with one of the killers and their conversation is a key motivation. Not only does Mickey argue against horror movies, when the debate takes a turn over the merits of the movie sequel, Randy proclaims that they "suck" while Mickey staunchly defends them (quick tip: you'll find that anybody in a *Scream* movie who makes some kind of point about violent film influence and/or expresses an interest in making movies should be ushered straight to the front of the suspect line-up; Mickey ticks both boxes). Mickey even continually brings up the sequel topic throughout the film, trying to find an example of a superior sequel that even Randy can't refute. Mickey's so adamant because, of course, he's trying to make a sequel himself.

At the end, when Mickey reveals himself to Sidney, he explains his master plan to her, James Bond-villain style: when he gets caught and put on trial, he plans on employing a "the movies made me do it" defense. He envisions the trial will become a media sensation that will have the moral majority crowd rally in his defense (more O.J. Simpson influence on the *Scream* series here). Frankly, his plan is ridiculous—even Mrs. Loomis says so when she sells him out and blows him away with her handgun—but it does tell us a lot about what

Mickey and *Scream 2* itself are trying to say.

It turns out Mickey doesn't actually believe in what he's been (and plans to continue) espousing—if he did, he wouldn't be presenting his plans as *how he's going to* blame the movies, he would just blame the movies. He doesn't say "the movies made me do it, Sid. They looked so fun, I wanted to do it myself." His argument at the beginning of the movie was just a set up for his grand scheme. He speaks of his would-be supporters in a contemptuous, "what fools" tone as he plans on manipulating them (either it's just Mickey, or Kevin Williamson makes an error here when Bible-belt Republicans are cited as being in this camp; the most famous contemporaneous attempts at censoring violent media certainly weren't the exclusive domain of American conservatives). Rather than make a real statement, Mickey simply thinks he's found the right alibi to get away with the perfect crime. If anything, Mickey really wants to prove how easy it is to exploit people's scapegoating.

Scream 2 wants us to consider that taking the "blame the movies" stance is essentially enabling someone like Mickey; it takes responsibility away from the culprit and puts it on innocent people, in this case the artists and audiences that enjoy a good thrill from a horror movie. Mickey is a sociopath (he wants to be a filmmaker but doesn't at all mind selling out the medium and his supposed passion so he can run his scheme) that thinks he can take advantage of society's self-reflection.

There's someone else in *Scream 2* that seeks to exploit media, but at least he has an ostensible justification. This is none other than Cotton Weary (still one of Liev Schreiber's more recognizable roles), the man Sidney had wrongfully accused of killing her mother a year before the events of the first *Scream*. Now free, Cotton hounds Sidney throughout *Scream 2* for a joint interview—first with Gale Weathers, but then, becoming more ambitious, with Diane Sawyer. He gets increasingly agitated at Sid's persistent refusals.

It serves *Scream 2* well that the only instance in the first *Scream* in which we get a glimpse of Cotton is through a television screen: a news clip using file footage of Cotton in handcuffs and an orange prisoner jumpsuit being led into a police car (it's amazing that Schreiber received billing for this single shot whose length is measured in literally seconds). For the year preceding (and probably even after) the events of *Scream*, this was the image Cotton Weary had in public: a criminal. It's this experience that taught Cotton that video, film and other media are what shapes perceived reality.

The first time we see Cotton in *Scream 2* is through the television, as well. Cotton is being interviewed (the host is Kevin Williamson in a cameo) about his experience and feelings about being wrongfully accused. It's the first step in his campaign to help clear his name: though Gale Weathers had advocated for his innocence before, if *The Woodsboro Murders* and *Stab* stick to the events shown in *Scream* as closely as it appears they do from what we see of them on-screen, Cotton likely never makes an appearance in either, and if he does, it's most likely as a recreation of that file footage clip of him in police custody.

Cotton seeks to erase, or at least overwhelm, that clip from the public's collective memory, but images die hard. What's more, though, discovering the power video and film have on people's perception of reality, he sees this as an opportunity not just for vindication but also for glory. If a little clip can make him a criminal, then a media publicity push can make him a hero, or a star.

Cotton Weary makes a pretty fantastic red herring; he not only has a genuine grievance against Sidney, he also has a vested interested in trying to alter reality. There could have very easily been an alternate ending in which Cotton is the killer, trying to create a sequel in which he gets to be the hero (the sexual themes would either require Mrs. Loomis still be around, too, or to be simply resolved by Derek's actions and sacrifice).

In the end, though, Cotton doesn't need to (even if he is creepy enough that we're still not entirely convinced he wouldn't or couldn't). Sidney, held hostage by Mrs. Loomis, finally relents to Cotton's offers for a joint interview, and Cotton then hits Mrs. Loomis with a bullet. Afterward, when the hungry press again crowds around Sidney, she points them to Cotton, telling them he's the hero. Cotton gets both his vindication and glory as the cameras gather around him, taking new images of Cotton the hero to replace the one of Cotton the criminal.

Sidney handing the cameras off to Cotton is a sign of her continuing exhaustion with media and pretty much all forms of altering reality. Not only has she been the object of numerous news reports, books and even a feature film, she's now twice been targeted in attempts to turn life into a horror movie.

Earlier in the movie, we see Sidney try to take solace in a different form of expression: she is cast in a stage play. She plays the role of Cassandra, the mythic Greek prophet who foresaw her own death but could do nothing to stop it. Unlike the killers who seek to change their reality into how they see fit, Sidney enters the world of the play to gain a new perspective on reality as it is—Gus, her stage director (a welcome cameo by David Warner) tells her that the stage is a battleground for the soul. Cassandra goes through a similar experience of impending doom, and as Sidney plays her she gets to live through Cassandra's madness as she resigns herself to her fate. It gives Sidney the perspective to choose how she wants to emotionally deal with her plight, to give into it like Cassandra does or to fight against it or avoid it. Sidney goes for the latter.

Scream 2 ends on a bittersweet note, as justice is restored: Mickey's grand scheme foiled, Mrs. Loomis destroyed, Cotton's unequivocal exoneration, among other things. But there's a sense that the damage has been done: Sidney walks off alone, having lost more friends and, this time, someone who truly loved her. What's more, some of the tears in the fabric of the *Scream* reality are starting to show, and the horror movie the killers work to bring about is gaining ground. There's always another horror sequel around the corner.

Part III—
SCREAM 3

Roman's Hollywood Horror

In *Scream 2*, the one major difference between our real world and the Real World of the *Scream* universe was that *Scream* itself existed in our world in the form of a movie. With the advent of *Stab*, it would seem that the *Scream* universe had found a way to—partially—reconvene with our own. The events of *Scream 2* would, of course, be another diverging point, but we could assume that there would be a *Stab 2* that would keep reality together.

Something funny happens when *Scream 3* starts, however. We learn that apparently the *Stab* movies are successful enough (we can only assume that they're as successful and influential as *Scream* is) that they've inspired Hollywood to go right ahead and greenlight *Stab 3: Return to Woodsboro* without it having any basis in reality. They're going to take the real characters of Sidney, Dewey and Gale and make up an entirely fictional story around them.

The implications this has on the *Scream* universe are huge. The first is that it has inspired and enabled yet *another* killer to take up the Ghostface mantle. Second, and maybe even greater, is that the horror movie world that's been rolling since the first *Scream* has now snowballed into something that just might be unstoppable. What chance does the Real World have if *Stab* movies can get produced without being based on actual incidents; altering the perceptions to the actual people in it? For instance, we learn that Gale is the killer in *Stab 3*. Gale is not the killer of *Scream 3*. The events of *Stab 3* are not the events of *Scream 3*. The events of *Stab 3* don't even exist! Because of this, the universe of *Scream* is closer to tearing itself apart from *our* reality than ever before, and it's all the more easier for the killer to succeed in killing Sidney and fulfilling his slasher movie-inspired brand of justice.

Adding to the madness is the fact that Ghostface is now targeting the very players involved in the production of *Stab 3* as if a *Stab* movie couldn't be supported by the universe if it didn't have a *Scream* equivalent in *our* reality. First on the chopping block is the long suffering Cotton Weary, who was due to have a cameo in *Stab 3*, and the production is shut down when *Stab 3* stars Sarah Darling (90s icon Jenny McCarthy) and Tom Prinze (Matt Keeslar), playing the *Stab* version of Dewey, are killed as well.

Who is the killer this time around? It's the director, of course, Roman Bridger (Scott Foley). He's started this latest Ghostface killing spree in order to draw Sidney out of hiding and kill her. It turns out Roman is Sid's half-brother, a long lost illegitimate son to Maureen Prescott. Maureen turned Roman away when he tracked her down some years ago, and in his bitterness he decided to secretly film her affairs with other men—and when he showed Billy Loomis the tape featuring her and his father Mr. Loomis, Roman inadvertently set this whole horror show into motion. Roman takes credit for Maureen's murder and now wants to kill Sidney, as well as frame her for the rest of his murders on the set of *Stab 3*. Jealous of Sidney's life as Maureen's child that was denied him, Roman stages this murder spree as the last of a trilogy which will culminate in his retribution.

You'll notice right off the bat that this is another reprise of the battle of the sexes that was waged in the first *Scream*. Roman is trying to kill Sidney for representing his rejection by a woman, and Sidney wins out again because her need for survival outweighs his need for acceptance. This is Billy/Mrs. Loomis all over again. Readers will note that the *Scream 3* section is the shortest of this book. This is not necessarily to say that there's less under the surface of *Scream 3* compared to its brethren, but that it covers territory already well-covered previously in the series.

New writer Ehren Kruger deserves credit, though, for being able to take over the reins from Kevin Williamson and craft a tale that may not bring a whole lot new to the table, but is at least properly in keeping with the themes and spirit of its lineage. Some sequels can't even do *that* (*Terminator 3: Rise of the Machines*, I'm looking in your direction here).

What *is* new this time around is the Hollywood setting and the "Trilogy" theme. *Scream 3* is ostensibly one of those "the gang goes to a wacky new location" sequels (see *A Very Brady Sequel, Star Trek IV: The Voyage Home, Rugrats in Paris*), but the story heading to Hollywood is actually not random at all; in fact, it's perfectly in keeping with the series.

Fitting for a grand finale, *Scream 3* treats Hollywood as The Source, where these reality-bending fantasies are all coming from. Not only is *Stab* being produced here, it's also apparently the origin of *Scream*'s sexual story. It turns out Maureen Prescott was trying to make it as an actress for a few years, and was introduced to the Casting Couch: directors and producers sleeping with young nubile actresses in exchange for parts. Horror producer John Milton (genre favorite Lance Henriksen) expected this of Maureen, but she refused, and she was apparently raped by him in return. Maureen subsequently fled Hollywood, but her lesson was learned: in order to get ahead in the world, she had to sleep around. And so "Maureen Prescott the Slut" was born.

In *Scream 3*'s Hollywood world of 2000, the Casting Couch is alive and well, and is presented as a kind of machine that turns innocents into bitter cynics. Jennifer Jolie (a lively Parker Posey), cast as *Stab 3*'s version of Gale, is a chain-smoking neurotic that off-handedly mentions she slept with Roman. Angelina Tyler (Emily Mortimer) won the part of *Stab 3*'s Sidney after Tori Spelling left, and we get to see her go from quiet and sensitive to a temperamental harpy at the end when she reveals that she'd had sex with Milton in order to get the part. Even Carrie Fisher makes a cameo as a file-keeping Hollywood burnout in which she jokes around that George Lucas gave the part of Princess Leia to the actress who slept with him.

Scream 3 presents Hollywood as a place that revels in its artifice and never takes anything seriously. Scream argued that filmmakers hadn't taken their horror movies seriously enough to even bother *trying* to make good ones anymore, and Scream 3 showcases this firsthand: the cast and crew are almost entirely resigned to the fact that they're making a "bad movie," and when faced with the Stab 3 production being shut down, the only defense Roman can muster is along the lines of "will killing horror movies make the psychos of the world retire?" No, says Scream 3, but aim a little higher and maybe the genre wouldn't be judged so harshly (on a side note, what did I say about characters who are aspiring filmmakers who argue about film persecution again?).

This lack of seriousness is also reflected in the tone of Scream 3. The series has always stuck to a "fun" kind of scariness, but Scream 3 goes still more lighthearted. Comic relief abounds, including random cameos—in addition to Carrie Fisher, Kevin Smith's Jay and Silent Bob characters make an appearance, too. The *Scooby-Doo* comparison to *Scream* has been there since the beginning, and *Scream 3* seems to specifically evoke it as its last act takes place in a vast mansion complete with a spooky basement and secret passageways. Reality is cast further into the wind, as Ghostface now possesses the ability to mimic any of the other characters' voices through an electronic voice box with magic Hollywood technology (a reflection of how *Stab* imitates *Scream*). Because it deals in the business of fantasies, Hollywood and the people behind it live in a kind of fantasy world itself, to the point of cartoonish excess.

Sidney is reminded of the power of Hollywood fantasies and how their influence can bleed into reality when she visits the *Stab 3* set and finds a remarkable recreation of Woodsboro, including a replica of her own house. The subsequent chase scene in this faux Woodsboro even mimics shots from the first *Scream*. Remember that Roman is trying to bring his movie (in *Scream 3*, not just *Stab 3*) full-circle with the events of *Scream* because he's gunning to create a final act in a trilogy. As grand finales often come with game-changing major character deaths, it tips the odds of Sidney's death or survival more in Roman's favor.

Unfortunately for Roman, *Scream 3* isn't the story of how Sidney goes insane with a lust for revenge against Milton and kills the cast of *Stab 3*. Rather, it's the story of how Sidney, Gale and Dewey venture to The Source of the horror movie world that's been threatening to take over their lives and finally end it by killing the director.

Dewey and Gale: A Real Life Movie Romance

This book hasn't yet had a whole lot of discussion of the relationship between two of the most important characters of the series: Dewey and Gale. Because they have more prominence in *Scream 3* and their romance culminates in Dewey proposing to Gale at the end of the film, it would appear that this is an appropriate moment to bring them up.

We've talked of Gale's function in the *Scream* universe, but not so much of Dewey. On a surface level, Dwight "Dewey" Riley's persistent survival throughout the series is a kind of extended joke. As the goofy, inexperienced deputy of the Woodsboro police force (he's only 25 years old in *Scream*), Dewey's not the guy you would expect to make it out alive at the end of a slasher flick. In fact, he wasn't originally planned to survive *Scream*, either—he proved popular enough with test audiences that Wes Craven opted to insert the shot of him alive and being led out on a stretcher at the end of the movie. *Scream 2* pulls the same conceit—Dewey ends up surviving an even hairier knife slashing by Ghostface. Dewey's presence as the *Scream* series goes on asks what would happen if one of those minor comic relief characters in a slasher movie managed to survive—and keep surviving. What would happen to his character?

I described this as a "joke" earlier, but it's one of the innovations that *Scream* brought to the horror genre (that still hasn't been wholly duplicated to this extent): a recurring ensemble cast. Provided they survive, the players in *Scream* come back for more. The only exceptions have been Joel from *Scream 2* and Detective Kincaid (Patrick Dempsey) from *Scream 3*, whose characters wouldn't have much of a place in the subsequent films anyway. For Sidney, Gale, Dewey, Randy, and Cotton, though, we get to see how the real-life horror movies the killers have wrought have affected their lives. This is a reversal of the standard slasher movie trope in which the killer is the real star of the show: this time it's the heroes that "just won't stay dead" while the killer is interchangeable.

As for Dewey, we get to see him gradually evolve into a more confident, competent man, all while retaining a core Dewey goofiness. This is in no small part due to his romantic relationship with Gale Weathers. The two are almost polar opposites but wind up complimenting each other well because of this—in *Scream 3* they have already broken up once and throughout the film enter the process of getting back together, both because of their differences. Where Dewey is a good-hearted man of the law who could use some help with his insecurities, Gale is a take-no-shit career woman who could learn to lighten up and treat people with more respect.

I said before that Gale could never be the killer so long as she was fighting on the side of reality, and the same is true of Dewey. Whereas Gale works to find the truth, however unethically, Dewey seeks justice, however incompetently. Dewey brings heart to Gale and Gale brings brains to Dewey, and, if you'll forgive the cheesy expression, together they form a bond that fights for truth and justice for the sake of Sidney, who's become a kind of guardian of reality.

Any talk of Gale and Dewey would not be complete if it weren't for the delicious development that the real-life (as in *our* real life) actors that portrayed them, Courteney Cox and David Arquette, became romantically involved as well. This book won't speculate or go into their personal lives at all, but it's eyebrow-raising to note that the pair met on the set of the first *Scream*, married just before *Scream 3*, and went into a trial separation just before the release of *Scream 4*. It's just one more way that the *Scream* movies toy with fantasy and reality.

Dewey surprises Gale with a marriage proposal at the end of *Scream 3* and she accepts, in what is an absolute rarity for the horror genre: an unambiguous happy ending. Marco Beltrami's score takes a triumphant tone that it never has in the series before as Sidney enters her home, her faith in reality restored, visited by the only two people throughout the series that she could ever truly count on. She's confident enough to even leave the door opened, knowing she can face whatever comes through.

Of course, a decade later, something does.

Part IV—
SCREAM 4

The State of Horror in 2011

Ten years is a lot of time in the movie business, and in the 11 years between *Scream 3* and *Scream 4* much had happened in both horror and the rest of genre filmmaking. In the immediate aftermath of *Scream* a wave of post-modern horror flicks arose to capitalize on its success. This gave way to rip-offs such as *Urban Legend* (1998), which basically tried to treat urban legends the way *Scream* treated other horror movies, to more original fare such as *Final Destination* (1999), whose characters seemed to step outside the rules of *life itself* and had fate try to double-back and kill them after missing them the first time around (*Final Destination* also serves as a kind of in-joke for gore hounds; it's a movie series with such purity of purpose that it's like it cut out the middle-man and had the concept of death itself be the "killer"). Even sequels to well-established series such as *Halloween: H2O* (1998), *Bride of Chucky* (1998) and the long-awaited *Freddy Vs. Jason* (2003) took a page out of *Scream*'s bloody handbook.

Not too long after *Scream 3*, however, horror started to take a turn away from irony and deconstruction to venture into other pastures. As if answering *Scream*'s call to take itself more seriously as an art form, the horror genre seemed to (try to, at least) do exactly that in various new forms.

The most notable trends for horror in the first decade of the 2000s can be summed up thus:

- The rise of the "found footage" subgenre.
- Intense "torture porn" flicks emerge.
- Foreign horror invades.
- Remakes and reboots of classics run amok.

Going over this point by point:

"*Found footage*" was famously launched by the ultra-low budget *The Blair Witch Project* in 1999, and though it was noteworthy for its novel "masquerading as actual amateur footage" presentation, the effect was so polarizing in audiences that even its own sequel abandoned that approach the following year.

However, in a few years a new subgenre launched in *Blair Witch*'s wake. *Cloverfield* (2008), *Quarantine* (2009), *Paranormal Activity* (2009) and many others would take horrific and often supernatural events and present them to audiences as actual footage "found" after the characters that had taken it perished.

"*Torture porn*" is a derisive name used to describe any number of horror flicks in the 2000s that evoked scenes of intense violence, gore, or prolonged suffering in order to create a harrowing experience for the audience. Movies most often associated with the label include *Hostel* (2003), the *Saw* series starting in 2004, *The Devil's Rejects* (2005) and *Captivity* (2007), but the term is used pretty much whenever someone feels disgusted by a piece of work.

Foreign horror has often been a key component of the genre, such as the Italian *giallos* of the 70s. In the 2000s, though, two new nations were put on the horror map: Japan and France.

Japanese horror movies were often of the supernatural variety and, rather than simply haunt a house or place, often were contained within a piece of technology, such as *Ring* (1998), whose monstrous ghost would spread via videotape.

Japanese horror sensations found Western mainstream acceptance in the form of remakes, such as *The Ring* (2002), *The Grudge* (2004), and *Pulse* (2005).

French horror films were more likely to be put under the "torture porn" umbrella with their penchant for being intense and violent, but often had original concepts and genuine suspense. *Inside* (2007), for instance, was about a pregnant woman battling against a sinister and deranged intruder who designed to steal her fetus. *High Tension* (2003), *Them* (2007) and *Martyrs* (2008) were also notable French horror releases.

That's not to say other nations didn't get a shot at horror: *Let the Right One In* (2006) from Sweden (remade as *Let Me In* in the US in 2010) gave us a look at the life of a vampire child, *REC* (2005), the original Spanish version of *Quarantine*, and the UK's *The Descent*, among others, made waves as well.

Remakes became a burgeoning trend throughout Hollywood in the 2000s but hit horror particularly hard. Remakes began being made so soon after their preceding film or series that a new term was coined to accommodate these early remakes: *reboot*. It seemed no cow was too sacred to tip: almost literally every successful horror franchise of the prior few decades got the new treatment, sometimes changing the story quite a bit (such as Rob Zombie's 2007 version of *Halloween*) or leaving it nearly untouched (think *The Omen* 2006). All of them were given a new, 21st century aesthetic.

Out of all these trends, there seemed to be one major theme that united them all: utter sincerity through intensity, nihilism, or hopelessness. In reaction to *Scream*, the horror genre took a few turns to become a much more serious genre than it had become in the late 80s and early 90s. With *Scream*'s return, what did it have to say about it all?

The Unexpected: The New Cliché

It's finally happened. As we return to the universe of *Scream* we find that it is no longer The Real World. Something's off.

The first major sign is that it's no longer easy to tell when *Stab* ends and *Scream* begins, which *Scream 4* uses to its advantage in a double fake-out opening in which we think we're watching *Scream 4* but are actually watching *Stab 6*, which is playing on the TV in front of two young women. When one of them suddenly whips out a knife and slams it into the other girl's torso, we find out that we're actually watching *Stab 7*, which is playing on the TV in front of two *other* girls.

So... are we in *Scream* now, or is this another *Stab*? We suspect we're in the film proper as the new scene seems to last a while, but until the animated *Scream 4* title card blazes across the screen we can't be 100% sure.

The oddness doesn't stop there. As *Scream 4* develops, we find that the characters are dumber: two hilariously inept bumbling cops, an idiot publicist who gets out of her car when she should be staying put and dialing for help, and everybody seems to wander off on their own in the dead of night when they all know there's a mad killer out there. The new teens are more callous than ever, going out to have a *Stab*-themed party in the middle of a killing spree that's claimed the life of one of their friends. The gore has ramped up to downright unrealistic levels: one scene has entire walls splashed with blood in a matter of minutes. Ghostface is now probably a foot taller than the actual killers that wear the costume. And to top it all off, our heroes Sidney, Gale, and Dewey are now dealing with the sixth and seventh serial killers in their lives. This isn't reality anymore. It looks like the *Scream* world has finally been transformed into the Movie Universe the killers have always chased after.

Scream 4's cinematography and *mise-en-scène* support this notion, as well. Where the *Scream* trilogy employed a naturalistic look (of course, it was in The Real World), *Scream 4* takes a more stylistic approach. The colors are muted somewhat, and the filmmakers apply bloom lighting throughout. Sunny windows are rectangles of big splashy vaseline whiteness and shiny surfaces (such as the blades of the knives) have a fuzzy resonance. For much of its running time, *Scream 4* is shot as if it were an extended dream sequence. The editing, too, is more hyper-active, though not in the way you might expect. Though it doesn't employ the Michael Bay-esque shaky-cam or rapid-fire cuts, *Scream 4* feels overly efficient, as if there were a dearth of establishing shots. Cuts happen too soon and scenes seem like they don't get a chance to breathe. There's a sense that the movie is moving just a little *too fast*, like a feature film slightly edited and time-compressed in order to fit into a predetermined timeslot. The real world slice-of-life moments are excised in favor of only those that serve the Movie Universe's narrative.

But if our heroes had destroyed all of the killers, including the director in Hollywood (read: The Source), how could the Movie Universe have taken over? There are two answers. The first is that since *Scream 3*, Hollywood never stopped making *Stab* movies. The aborted *Stab 3* was reborn as a dramatization of the events that happened in *Scream 3*, and as we see in the opening to *Scream 4*, four *more* sequels were made after that. Remember that the more sequels to *Stab* that are made without a *Scream* counterpart in *our* world, the more the *Scream* universe diverges from reality. Luckily, after *Stab 3* Sidney sued the producers of the *Stab* franchise to stop them from using her likeness in any more *Stab* movies, so from *Stab 4* onwards the series took on entirely fictional stories with new, made-up characters. Sidney's litigious actions helped mitigate the damage to the *Scream* world's grasp on reality.

Eleven years onward, though, the proverbial straw has broken the camel's back and the *Scream* world is plunged into the kind of horror fantasy that Billy Loomis tried to create so long ago: a new killer has emerged in Woodsboro and is stalking and killing teens in the Ghostface persona, not coincidentally as Sidney arrives back in town to promote her new self-help book *Out of the Darkness*. With the *Stab* movies now having nothing to do with our heroes, though, what has enabled the new killer? Why now?

The first hint is the glimpse that *Scream 4* gives us of what's become of *Stab* in the meantime: it's always been an alternate-reality take on *Scream*, but now we get to see an alternate-reality take on what *Scream* might have turned out if it hadn't ended and had simply continued pumping out sequels throughout the 2000s. The *Stab* movies have become ridiculous as the installments piled up: *Stab 7* starts off with characters watching *Stab 6*, which featured a cheating teleporting killer (or perhaps there were two Ghostfaces out in the open; the scene ends before it becomes clear), and we hear of the infamous *Stab 5* in which the killer utilized time travel.

A quick note about what we see of *Stab 6* and *7* is that they're both inside jokes subverting the most common expectations of Lame Things That Would Probably Happen in a 21st century *Scream* movie. *Stab 6* stars Shenae Grimes and Lucy Hale encountering a Facebook stalker (the movie misses an opportunity to have one of the girls, instead of dialing 911, take to Twitter to tell everyone, *"Help! Killr on fone wat shuld I do! XD"*). *Stab 7* subsequently stars Anna Paquin and Kristen Bell and has them spouting inane meta commentary about the state of the horror genre (now here's a thought: are Anna Paquin, Kristen Bell and the others actually starring in *Stab* or are they playing other actresses *playing* these *Stab* characters?). Of course, *Scream 4* continues with the self-referential chatter, but uses *Stab 7* to poke fun at itself.

Scream 4 tells us that most movies aren't built to have an extended series of sequels attached, and the more you try to force sequels on a concept that just doesn't warrant it, the more ridiculous things become. Michael Myers eventually became the subject of a shadowy cult, Freddy Krueger eventually started killing people with Nintendo Power Gloves, Jason was launched into space and the Leprechaun went *Back 2 da Hood*. Being part four in a slasher movie series, *Scream 4* itself is pretty ridiculous in concept: being the target of seven different serial killers is not something that has happened to anyone in the history of the world, ever.

But absurd plot developments in advanced sequels in themselves aren't the reason why a new killer has been able to come around after so long: it's what happens to a movie series afterward. The *Stab* series is ripe for a reboot.

Kill Jill

Imagine it's 2011 and there's a guy in his 30s, a casual horror fan, who plops down on his sofa after a long day at work and turns on the cable box to see if there's anything good on. Let's say his name is Bob.

Oh look, Bob thinks. *Halloween is on!*

Changing the channel over, the guy is disappointed to see that it's not John Carpenter's *Halloween* of 1978 playing, but rather Rob Zombie's 2007 update.

Flipping back through the guide, Bob stumbles across something else that catches his eye. *Texas Chain Saw Massacre, I've always wanted to see that one*. But, of course, when Bob switches the station over it's not Tobe Hooper's 1974 shocker playing, it's the 2003 *Texas Chainsaw Massacre*. Bob didn't really want to see the do-over without first getting a viewing of the original, but it's getting late and he's tired of channel-surfing, so Bill settles for the new *Texas Chainsaw*.

In the 2000s and beyond, movie series that get one (or more) too many sequels and wear out their welcome don't just merely die off. They get rebooted. The first decade of the 21st century did for the remake what the 1980s did for the sequel. *Friday the 13th Part 2* from 1981 showed Hollywood that, yes, you *can* just make the same movie over again and people will come back to see it, and a new era began of sequel after sequel, not only for horror, but for all of the movie industry. The 2000s proved that you no longer had to even pretend you're packaging a new story, as *Planet of the Apes* 2001 and *Texas Chainsaw Massacre* 2003 helped usher in a new era of remakes and "re-imaginings" (thank Tim Burton for coining that one).

It was *Batman Begins* in 2005 where people started using the term "reboot": *Batman & Robin* was a mere eight years earlier, and *Begins* was less a remake of *Batman* (1989) than it was a hitting of the reset button to get the Bat franchise away from the camp and absurdity it had grown into by the late 90s. Its success, and especially that of its blockbuster sequel *The Dark Knight* (2008) proved you no longer had to even wait for the franchise to grow old before dipping back in the well again: *The Incredible Hulk* (2008) rebooted *Hulk* (2003), and even the blockbuster *Spider-Man* series earned a reboot in *The Amazing Spider-Man* (2012), just five years after its last installment. Just as sequel-itis hit horror particularly hard in the 80s, so too did the horror genre oblige in riding the big kahuna reboot wave. Name a popular horror hit from the 80s and someone could point you to a 2000s remake.

In 2011, it looked like it was *Scream*'s turn. Though it would stay in continuity with the prior trilogy and Sidney, Gale, and Dewey would return for this installment, *Scream 4* was marketed as a *Star Trek: Generations*-style passing-of-the-torch tale to a new generation cast, who would carry on the series through a new trilogy (the film is even titled *Scream 4: Next Generation* in Japan). Emma Roberts played Jill, Sidney's cousin, and in interviews and magazine covers she expounded on Jill's role as "The New Sidney" and the apparent new face of *Scream* for Generation Y.

So in *Scream 4*, the new killer emerges in Woodsboro because the *Stab* series has gone on too long for its own good, and the mentality of the new era demands a reboot. *Scream 4* is definitely set up this way: Jill is the new Sidney, her friends Olivia

(Marielle Jaffe) and Kirby (Hayden Panettiere) collectively form the new Tatum (Olivia represents Tatum's feminine attractiveness, Kirby her tomboy side), movie-club geeks Charlie and Robbie (Rory Culkin and Erik Knudsen, respectively) are the new Randy, Deputy Judy Hicks (Marley Shelton) the new Dewey, and Jill's ex-boyfriend Trevor the new Billy. You can even make a case for Sidney's ruthless publicist, Rebecca (Alison Brie), being a version of Gale (public relations is often seen as "the other side" of the same coin as journalism).

The first big difference with the new *Scream* is that the battle of the sexes has finally been retired. When a female character shoots a man's genitals late in the film, you get the feeling that the women of *Scream 4* are no longer all that existentially concerned that men are going to kill them. Even the opening underlines this: instead of focusing on a pair of lovers like the prior *Scream* movies, *4*'s beginning gives us three pairs of female friends instead.

The movie even uses the prior battle of the sexes motif from the original trilogy to misdirect the audience: Trevor is set up much like Billy; we might see his persistence to get back with Jill, his ex, as stalker-like behavior in light of Billy's actions in the first *Scream*, but in the end we find that Jill isn't threatened by him at all—in fact, she loves the attention.

Scream 4 presents androgyny as a kind of truce between the sexes: Kirby is an obvious tomboy, wearing masculine clothes and a closely cropped hairstyle. Charlie sports long hair that, while definitely not a new thing for men, is the first of its kind in Scream (and Charlie's particular style of long locks wasn't really a hip thing in 2011). Trevor has a kind of metrosexual look and demeanor to him that Billy didn't. Robbie suggests homosexuality as the only sure-fire way to survive a horror movie in the new decade, and he even claims to be so after being stabbed by Ghostface (whether it's true or not is up to us to decide, but on a second watch it works for his character). Once again there are two killers in Scream 4, and one of them is male and one of them is female, but this time it represents an androgynous side to Ghostface, rather than a female having to become a man in order to kill like in Scream 2. Apparently, whatever hang-ups the new generation has, they're not psychosexual anymore.

The second big difference between the new cast and the original is that when it comes to dealing with the killer, well, the new guys kind of suck. As mentioned before, the new characters are more stupid and heartless than the original crew ever was in even their worst moments. It was a challenge for Ghostface to kill most of the victims in *Scream*, leading to many thrilling chase scenes and moments when the characters would resist or try to fight back. The new characters in *Scream 4*, on the other hand, fall like dominoes, and it's only Sidney (and at one point, Gale) that gives Ghostface a run for his money in this one. Kirby comes across as intelligent, but her smartassery sometimes has her, too, crossing the line into straight-up callousness (she's present at "Stab-a-thon," a marathon party celebrating the *Stab* movies, even though one of her friends was just brutally murdered before her eyes recently). Jill, too, comes off kind of distant and a little spoiled, though the audience probably suspects that, since Jill is set up as the new Final Girl, she's going through a character arc where she will eventually come to appreciate what Sidney's been through at the end.

...Except we get to the end and Ghostface is unmasked before a cornered Sidney, and the killer is none other than Jill herself. Just as the marketing for *Scream* misled people into thinking Drew Barrymore was the star, the marketing for *Scream 4* misled people into thinking Emma Roberts is the star. Just as the true twist to *Scream* was that we weren't actually watching a horror movie as we knew it, the true twist to *Scream 4* is that we weren't actually watching a *reboot* at all, it was all Jill's devious plan (even the film's logo, whose spelling is stylized "SCRE4M," depicts how the movie is a sequel hidden under the guise of a reboot). She's collaborated with Charlie, but she double-crosses him and sets him up, along with the innocent Trevor, to take the blame for the killings. Notice there was misdirection as to Charlie's role in *Scream 4*, as well. He was presented as a new Randy, but there already was a new Randy in the form of Robbie. There wasn't an apparent "new Stu" until the end—it's Charlie.

With Charlie and Trevor out of the way and framed to look like the new Stu and Billy, Jill lays it all out on the table: envious of Sidney's fame as a chronic survivor and subject of three famous movies, Jill's set this 'reboot' into motion so that she can become the new Final Girl, and she can kill Sidney and take her place and instantly gain her fame, sympathy, and admiration. She stabs Sidney to apparent death, and Jill proceeds to self-mutilate herself to convincingly look the part of a survivor.

Jill may well be the most evil character in the *Scream* world. Take away the fact that they're a killer from the other villains and what do you get?

Billy and Roman are hurt, abandoned sons. Mrs. Loomis is a grieving mother. Stu is a secretly sensitive guy who would do anything to fit in. Charlie is lonely and desperate to do *anything* for the love of a woman. Even Mickey wanted to demonstrate a point. Take away the fact that she's a killer, however, and Jill is still evil: she's a fraud, a cheat. Jill is a conniving sociopath who would sell out any of her supposed loved ones in order to pursue her selfish interests. Jill covets and feels entitled to the Final Girl position. She wants to be The New Sidney, but instead of earning it like Sidney has, she creates fake circumstances in order to try to achieve it. Jill isn't "real." The unreality of *Scream 4*'s Movie Universe reflects the fakery that is Jill and everything she stands for.

This is essentially the fear and knee-jerk reaction movie fans feel when their favorite works are put through the reboot machine: the prior series is "killed" and a new movie is put in its place. But while the original earned its status, the remake simply rides on the name and goodwill of the original. John Carpenter's *Halloween* no longer completely owns the story of Michael Myers and Laurie Strode. In 2011, it has to, at best, share that story with Rob Zombie's 2007 *Halloween*. John Carpenter's film came out of nowhere to earn a place for itself in the genre movie canon. Rob Zombie's film, though, burst onto the scene with great fanfare as "the new *Halloween!*"

Notice how, when a remake goes badly, people will talk of how the remake "ruined" the story. It's the sentiment that the remake "takes" the place of the original as the keeper of that story and has a responsibility to live up to it, or barring that, to play as a kind of "tribute" to the original, acknowledging the original's superiority. If we remember Bob from the beginning of the chapter and his situation of having all the classic movies he expects to see turning out to be their remakes instead, it's easy to see how one gets the feeling that original movies, being considered "old" and obsolete, are taken out back and put out of their misery, and replaced by usurpers.

Scream 4 expresses a despair at the productivity of the reboot-machine in the scene in which Kirby is being quizzed by the killer, and when he asks her to name a particular horror remake, she rapid-fires a seemingly never-ending list of titles that is at first a little funny, but as the list goes on, and on, and *on*, and the desperation and tension rise in Kirby's voice, it becomes sad. Virtually *every successful horror movie or series of the past couple of decades has been remade,* their stories and their place in popular culture taken from them by others wanting to make a quick buck; and in a way, they've been killed.

It's important to note that Jill is specifically a bad, inferior remake of Sidney, a pretender to the throne, a soulless cash-in looking to score easy fame. *Scream 4* doesn't hate remakes any more than *Scream* hated horror movies. There are plenty of good remakes: *The Fly* (1986), for instance, or Carpenter's own *The Thing* (1982). Both of these examples were honest attempts at taking a different approach to the original films. The key is that they don't try to replace the original; rather, they found and earned their own story. This book has picked on Rob Zombie, but I do think that, however controversial the results, he honestly attempted to create a movie that complimented, rather than replaced, Carpenter's *Halloween* (The Weinstein Company, who commissioned the remake, probably had other designs, though). *A Nightmare on Elm Street* (2010), on the other hand, was greenlit entirely because *Friday the 13th* (2009) had a splashy opening weekend and the Freddy Krueger remake was put on the fast-track in order to capitalize. Regardless of the cast and crew's intentions and efforts, the new *Nightmare* was created because the original needed replacing and there was money to be made.

So it seems, like so many reboots before her, that Jill has achieved her goal of becoming the Final Girl, The New Sidney, as the paramedics arrive and she's taken into an ambulance on a stretcher, and the screen fades to white... until at the hospital we learn that Sidney has survived. In an attempt to kill Sidney again, Jill winds up having a stand-off between her and The Originals Sid, Gale, and Dewey, and she is eventually defibrillated in the head and then shot in the heart by Sidney. In fact, the only survivor out of the new cast is Deputy Hicks, who *Scream 4* points out as actually being a part of Sidney's generation, having graduated in the same class.

Scream 4 observes that remade classic original pictures may not be so dead after all. If the "replacement" is truly inferior, their time in ownership of its story will eventually fade, and the original will return to its prominence. Even though *Scream 4* fades out with news reporters, unaware of the latest developments, announcing the heroic courage of Jill Roberts, *Scream*'s pillars of reality and the pursuit of truth and justice (Sidney, Gale, and Dewey) still stand; and Jill's post-mortem time in the spotlight, like any bad remake, will be fleeting.

The best remakes are the ones that earn their fame and recognition. Sidney lets Jill know this at the end when, having successfully fought off her own reboot and killed the "new trilogy" before it could really get going, she tells Jill's corpse how she broke the first rule of a remake: not to fuck with the original.

Meet the New Media,
Same as the Old Media

As pointed out earlier, *Scream* was the first major horror film of the information age, so it's only appropriate that *Scream 4* deals with the developments in new media in the series' decade-long slumber. In between *Scream 3* and *4* we've seen the rise of smartphones, Web 2.0, and social networking. Ostensibly we're more interconnected (and presumably safer) than ever.

Of course, this means *Scream* has to turn that sense of security on its head. Excepting Rebecca's inexplicable failure to realize she really, really ought to stay in her car and dial 911, the new technology only serves Ghostface at least as much as it repels him. He circumvents and exploits caller ID by simply stealing his victims' phones: the next victim(s) think their friend is calling them. More than that, getting his hands on his victims' phones gives the killer access to their friends' phone numbers and contact information, adding more potential names to the kill list. We find out in the opening scene that there is a Ghostface-voice app that lets anybody sound like the killer over the phone, making it that much easier for anybody to be the killer.

Even the safety of surveillance gets exploited by the killer, as Robbie wears a camera on his head that broadcasts to the web at all times. This means that there's less a chance for him to be cornered while he's "alone," but overlooks the fact that *the killer, too, knows exactly where he is at any given time*, and can simply wait for an opportune time to take him out. The camera makes Robbie just as vulnerable as it makes him safe.

The biggest cultural contribution the web has brought us in the oos, though, is social networking. Its most prominent appearance is in the hokey "Facebook stalker" opening to *Stab 6*, but its specter is all over *Scream 4*. Jill wants to become famous because of the inherent power and control it gives her over her relationships and general communication. Jill wants to live a life of sending out press releases and giving interviews in which her message (of her inherent greatness, surely) goes largely unchallenged. She wants to be The New Sidney by simply *saying* that she's The New Sidney. The unspoken assertion in *Scream 4* is that *Jill got her first taste of stardom through social networking*. Social networking allows Jill to present herself in whatever image she likes. She gets to rack up "friends" and treat them more like the fans she craves (Twitter even calls them "followers!"). While social networking allows for back-and-forth communication, it removes extemporaneousness: every message on Facebook is potentially an Official Statement. And if Jill doesn't like what somebody has to say about her? Just block them. Social networking has given the horror movie fantasy a powerful tool to infect the Real World.

Scream 4 supplants the Battle of the Sexes with a Battle of the Generations. Notice how in contrast to Jill presumably using new media to advance her fantasy world, Sidney uses a very old medium—a book—as her testimony of reality. Rebecca the publicist may not literally be Generation Y, but her conversation with Gale makes it clear who has seniority. As stated before, Gale works to find truth, while Rebecca's job involves entirely trying to spin the truth into something desirable for her client (and it's telling that Sidney winds up firing her in disgust). Notice that when we first see Gale in *Scream 4* she's going through a bad case of writer's block; it's because she's trying to write fiction and she's out of her element. Gale's role is on the side of reality. She finally gets her mojo back when she gets a chance to settle into her job as an investigator, trying to uncover the truth of the mystery killer.

In the end, the only new major character left standing is Deputy Hicks, and it's explicitly mentioned that she is actually from Sidney's generation. *Scream 4* isn't advocating the eradication of Generation Y or even necessarily the superiority of Generation X, but it uses the generational gap as another metaphor for the series' *fantasy vs. reality* theme and how things have changed over time. The characters of the original *Scream* trilogy had to deal with killers enabled by film and TV. The millennials of *Scream 4* must deal with sociopaths enabled by smartphones and social media. That none of the Generation Y cast survives *Scream 4* is a sign that they may still have to come of age.

There's a third generation present in *Scream 4*, actually: the baby boomers, as represented by Kate Roberts (Mary McDonnell), mother to Jill and aunt to Sidney. Kate's part is small, but there's a lot we can gleam from her presence: she comes across as well-meaning but aloof, and there's a noticeable distance between her and Jill even before we see Sidney discover Jill decry Kate over instant messenger (like Sidney using DeafTyper in the original *Scream* to hide conversations from her father, Jill uses the web to hide conversations from her mother). There's no father to speak of, and his absence likely fuels Kate's Prozac-like malaise. Though everybody is responsible for their own actions, *Scream* lays out that the Baby Boomers, however well-meaning, had failed their children (Jill is now the third killer with mother issues). Kate's last request before her death: to tell Jill she's sorry. It's too late; Jill's already become a monster.

I don't think *Scream 4* is an indictment against new media any more than *Scream* was an indictment against the telephone. New media has rightfully been heralded for the speed and accuracy with which it can shed light on reality: it's been said that the numerous revolutions against dictatorships in the late 00s and early 2010s might not have happened without it. *Scream 4* reminds us, though, that as long as we have an imperfect medium, deceit and lies can spread just as quickly and easily as the truth.

Surviving in a Post-Scream World

Some critics would have preferred if *Scream 4* had ended with Jill victorious, that the fade to white as Jill was carried into the ambulance was followed by closing credits and nothing more. That *Scream 4* provides a "second ending" that reverses Jill's fortune and has the good guys destroy her, they say, represents the film "chickening out" of what would have been a more unpredictable ending, one that would have had "guts."

Such sentiments, *Scream 4* says, are part of the problem. As stated before, the horror genre's reaction to *Scream*, after initially trying to recreate it, was to turn more serious, which isn't a bad thing at all. After a few years, though, what started out as a bid for a "back to basics" approach to provide a good, old fashioned scare turned into a race for authenticity, a kind of purity of form. This desire turned into a trend of nihilism and depravity that, while certainly not universal (*Cabin Fever* (2003) and the *Final Destination* sequels proved there was still a place for 'fun' horror), seemed prevalent enough to touch on almost every corner of the horror genre.

This trend almost single handedly gave rise to the "torture porn" label used to brand movies that seemed to dwell on suffering and gore, usually featuring captured victims being subjected to obscene cruelty, the idea being that the viewer gets to experience "pure" horror and disturbance.

The "found footage" subgenre, too, is largely fueled by this desire for authenticity. The entire presentation of found footage movies is made to exploit the mental association people make between video footage and objective reality. The killers of *Scream 4* try to exploit this when they reveal they've recorded the murders they commit. The videos convey authentic horror, but also further a hidden agenda: to turn Jill into a superstar. The movie misses a huge opportunity here, actually: there could have been a scene in which Jill herself is called and subsequently chased by Ghostface, and this incident later revealed as an act for the cameras.

This want for authenticity led a whole gaggle of horror films to embrace what many considered the ultimate horror: the monster winning. Horror film after horror film in the 2000s went for the "unpredictable" ending that "told it like it was" and "had guts." *Texas Chainsaw Massacre: The Beginning* (2006), *The Strangers* (2008), *The Grudge 2* (2006), most any *Saw* movie, the original ending of *The Descent* (2006), any found footage movie, and pretty much any French horror film all saw every last one of the protagonists biting the dust and succumbing to the horror.

Even movies outside of the horror genre started getting in on the action. 2007's Academy Award-winning *No Country for Old Men* interrupted its on-the-run-from-a-hitman story three-fourths of the way through by having its antagonist unceremoniously killed by random gangsters, while the hitman subsequently kills his wife, and the sheriff that's been tailing both of them throughout the film gives up and retires. There is no inherent justice to the universe, *No Country* tells us, and while that may be true, it's a sentiment that's been repeated countless times, especially in horror.

Not everyone embraced the nihilism. Roger Ebert slammed *Chaos*, a low-budget independent

2005 horror flick that all but remade Wes Craven's 1972 film *Last House on the Left* (which later got an *official* remake), only in *Chaos* evil triumphs. The director and producer of the film wrote an open letter in response to Ebert's review defending their film as a depiction of "real" evil, a reflection of the times. Ebert refuted this notion and maintained that if the world truly is such an evil place, that it needs catharsis in cinema more than ever.

Some films themselves commented on film depravity, such as Michael Haneke's *Funny Games* (2007), an American remake of Haneke's own foreign original (covering all bases, apparently), which presents itself as a thriller in which a family must fend off or escape a pair of sadistic teenage intruders. However, the film directly breaks the fourth wall and purposefully strips the family's terror of anything that could be considered thrilling and enjoyable until there is nothing left but the sheer horribleness of the events. As if taking the opening of *Scream 2* and injecting it with steroids, *Funny Games* seeks to punish those viewers that come to see horror movies in order to see someone die, by employing a "be careful what you wish for," motif.

In *Scream 4*, as Jill seems victorious in her devious plan for fame, this "first ending" appears in line with the values of the 2000s nihilistic horror film, in which evil exists, bad things happen and there's nothing you can do about it. But when we fade back into the hospital and Dewey lets Jill know that Sidney survived the ordeal, *Scream 4* finally says, "Enough," and pulls the rug out from underneath.

When Sidney, Gale and Dewey destroy Jill in the "second ending," they're destroying her 2000s horror move values along with her just as Sidney destroyed Billy's 1980s horror movie values. There's no point or value in simply pointing out that evil exists, *Scream 4* says, without any insight in how we deal with it. Justice may not be inherent to the universe, and maybe we won't get out alive after all, but if we're to even have a chance, it'll be hope and determination that will take us there.

Scream Echoes

In the fifteen years between *Scream* and *Scream 4*, the film series' influence has reached throughout popular culture, and the horror genre in particular has largely been in reaction to it the entire time.

Is that enough to justify this book, though? Why take the effort to analyze this one movie series? It's largely because *Scream* itself calls for this kind of introspection, not just in itself, or horror movies, but for our own lives as well. Self awareness is important, *Scream* says, because what we think we are saying and standing for may not be what we're actually doing.

Scream, too, isn't immune to having inadvertent themes. The series brings a kind of right-wing libertarian bent to horror that I'm still not convinced is wholly intentional. The killers all ultimately seek to shuck their personal responsibility elsewhere. Billy blames everything on Maureen Prescott. Stu blames peer pressure. Mickey wanted to officially blame it on the movies. Mrs. Loomis blames Sidney and her mother. Roman becomes irate when Sidney reminds him that it's him and only him who is responsible for his murderous actions. Probably the best example, Jill's entire motivation is her envy of the status Sidney has earned and the apparent unfairness that Sidney gets to be a hero and Jill doesn't; Jill seeks to rectify this situation, not by doing anything to earn it herself, but by stealing it from Sidney.

The *Scream* movies put Sidney in a constant struggle to assert her personal autonomy in the face of forces trying to get her to conform. The 80s slasher convention demands that Sidney be a virgin if she wants to survive. Billy wants her to be a "slut" in order to kill her. The sorority girls in *Scream 2* that court Sidney are all shallow replicas of each other and we suspect they'll try to convert Sidney, too, should she ever join. Sidney discovers Hollywood punished her mother for not conforming to the Casting Couch rules. And of course Jill wants to bring Sidney down from her class as a celebrity. In fact, *Scream 4* shows that not everybody in Woodsboro views Sidney with admiration: Olivia, for instance, refers to Sid as the "Angel of Death" and even Ghostface seems to be personally annoyed that Sidney has survived so many encounters. After Olivia's murder, bystanders outside the crime scene heckle Sidney, telling her it's her fault and that she shouldn't have come back. There's a sense of resentment there, as if it were wrong that Sidney survives so many murder attempts while those around her perish. It's as if Ghostface has taken it upon himself to try to kill her because *that's just not fair,* in order to "redistribute the survival" and allow someone new to be the Final Girl: Jill, who has put the events of *Scream 4* into motion herself. As Sidney defeats Jill and the other killers in the series, she exercises her liberty to live and act as she sees fit.

Whether these politics are intentional or not, it's through analysis, self reflection, and deconstruction that we gain the perspective to find messages like these. *Scream* asks us to, every now and then, step aside and take a good, long look at who we are, what we're doing, and where we're going. What you see of yourself might make you smile. It might make you scream.

Reference

♦ Clover, Carol J. <u>Men, Women, and Chain Saws: Gender in the Modern Horror Film.</u> Princeton: Princeton University Press, 1992.

♦ "Deconstruct." *Merriam-Webster.com.* Merriam-Webster, 2011.

♦ De Becker, Gavin. *The Gift of Fear: Survival Signs that Protect Us from Violence.* Boston: Little, Brown, 1997.

♦ Ebert, Roger. "Evil in film: To what end?" <u>Chicago Sun-Times</u> 25 August 2005.

♦ Handlen, Zack. "Gateways to Geekery: Slasher films." <u>The A.V. Club</u> 22 October 2009.

- Murray, Noel, Nathan Rabin and Scott Tobias. ""What Monster Could Have Done This?": Horror Films for Left-Wingers/ Horror Films For Right-Wingers." <u>The A.V. Club</u> 26 October 2006.

- "Satire." *Merriam-Webster.com*. Merriam-Webster, 2011.